VULNERABLE YOUTH
IN RESIDENTIAL CARE
PART II

J.D. van der Ploeg, P.M. van den Bergh, M. Klomp
E.J. Knorth & M. Smit
(eds.)

Vulnerable Youth
in
Residential Care

Part II
Clients, Staff and the System

Leuven-Apeldoorn

J.D. van der Ploeg, P.M. van den Bergh, M. Klomp, E.J. Knorth & M. Smit (eds.)
Vulnerable Youth in Residential Care
Part II : Clients, Staff and the System
Leuven/Apeldoorn
Garant, 1992 – First edition
227 p.; 24 cm
D/1992/5779/60
ISBN 90-5350-168-1
NUGI 725

Cover : Hedwige Dirkx

Garant
Tiensesteenweg 83, 3010 Leuven – Kessel-Lo (Belgium)
Koninginnelaan 96, 7315 EB Apeldoorn (The Netherlands)

CONTENTS:

6

SECTION II: MANAGEMENT ISSUES

Under the auspices of EUSARF, the European Scientific Association for Residential and Foster Care for Children and Adolescents

Executive Committee:
Prof. Dr. W. Hellinckx [Belgium]
Prof. Dr. S. Millham [Great Britain]
Prof. Dr. J.D. Van der Ploeg [The Netherlands]
Prof. Dr. E. Broekaert [Belgium]
Mrs Dr. H. Agathonos-Georgopoulou [Greece]
Prof. Dr. F. Casas Aznar [Spain]
Mrs H. Cleaver [Great Britain]
Prof. Dr. H.E. Colla-Müller [Germany]
Dr. M.J. Colton [Great Britain]
Dr. M. Corbillon [France]
Prof. Dr. P. Durning [France]
Dr. E.J. Knorth [The Netherlands]
Mrs Dr. J. Mehlbye [Denmark]
Mrs A. Vanden Berge [Belgium]

Acknowledgements:

Our work in preparing this book was supported by
The Ministry of Justice
The Ministry of Welfare, Public Health and Culture
Stichting Rijnstroom Beheer

1 Residential Care in Motion; Some Clinical and Management Issues

M. Klomp & E.J. Knorth

1.1 Introduction

Residential child care is a grave intervention. It can be considered a treatment option if the problems with a child in the home environment are so serious that the parents are unable to cope with them. The task which residential care sets for itself is therefore a large and difficult one.

Nevertheless, comparatively little is known about the way in which this help takes place. Hence it is important that we try to get a more precise picture of the processes of care involved, preferably based on results of process evaluation research (cf. Harinck & Smit, 1992).

Children in residential care have severe psycho-social problems; a specific approach is necessary to meet these problems and to create real possibilities for development and growth. It requires a residential social worker who can act with expertise and reflection and who has his heart in the right place. This might create a kind of a paradox: the social worker is faced with the task of developing a well thought-out and accounted-for treatment plan; but in its execution he should, as much as possible, break through the 'planned' way of working with the children and be as flexible as possible (Klomp & Van Oeffelt, 1978).

However in recent years the idea has gained ground that these two approaches are not opposed to each other: planning and goal-oriented action do not exclude creating a home environment that is as natural as possible. Moreover, it is so that planning and goal orientation are necessary issues in order to justify the social worker's interventions afterwards (cf. Bryer, 1988; Knorth & Smit, 1990).

Residential care is subject to changes. Retrenchments, for example, can be seen in many countries (cf. Colton & Hellinckx, 1992). Instead of having a paralysing effect in the field they challenge the creativity to maintain and improve the quality of residential care: the field is in constant flux and innovations are taking place everywhere (cf. Hellinckx, Broekaert, Vanden Berge & Colton, 1991).
In our opinion it is important that these new developments be explained and justified. This book can be seen as a contribution to this process. It contains a variety of articles on residential child care. They provide some insight into the 'black box' of the social care process, including new concepts and methods.

The entries are divided into two sections. In the first section clinical issues such as features of child psychopathology, assessment difficulties, helping maltreated children, social competence training, and working with the family are discussed. In the second part the focus is on management issues such as coping with crisis, stress and anxiety phenomena in the organization, training and supervision of staff members, system analysis, and program evaluation. We shall expound on the various chapters in turn.

1.2   The clients; clinical issues

In Part I of this book a number of questions concerning *assessment and treatment* of children and adolescents in residential care is reviewed.

In chapter 2 **Van der Doef** deals with a theoretical model, in which four frequently-occurring psychopathological 'diagnoses' in residential child care (namely: children with behaviourial disorders, anxiety disorders, attention deficit disorders and pervasive developmental disorders, i.e. autism) are compared. The model contains a classification and a treatment component. In the classification of the aforementioned problem types there are, according to Van der Doef, two fundamental questions under discussion: 1) should the disturbed interaction between child and environment primarily be regarded as a problem of assimilation or as a problem of accommodation? and 2) did the child (originally) have mainly cognitive or emotional problems? With regard to the treatment and especially to the daily living situation which is being created for these children in a treatment centre, one can say that either structuring the pedagogical situation or establishing a pedagogical relationship should get priority. Because the model is based upon psychological, psychiatric and pedagogical concepts, it offers an interesting frame for reflection on inter-disciplinary co-operation and theory development.

The following two contributions refer to the onset of a residential care process: the placement and intake phase. More specifically a description is presented of some of the *assessment difficulties* that can occur *at the beginning*.

Van der Laan brings up an urgent problem in the Netherlands. For a number of youths a place in a residential home is extremely difficult to find. This phenomenon is not unique to the Netherlands. It partially has to do with the reduced capacity in intramural youth care, a development that is seen in other parts of Europe as well (cf. Colton & Hellinckx, 1992). On the other hand, the author, based on his research of over 350 youths under court order who proved 'difficult to place', also found obscurities in the description of the care needed (by the placement officer) and in the profile of the help offered (by the residential setting), both of which contribute to stagnation in the placement process. Special attention is given to the problem of 'non-motivated' youths.

In the article by **Van den Bergh** a problem indicated briefly in the preceding chapter is expanded on: the quality of the diagnostic information given by the referring agent upon application. Using a questionnaire, the author examined the level of information contained in the written application reports regarding over 180 youths in three residential centres. He also asked the staff members for their judgement. The questionnaires as well as the staff data show that there are important gaps in the referral reports. Nonetheless placement decisions are taken. Van den Bergh tries to find out what is behind this. He also makes a proposal for a solution.

A substantial part of the children and adolescents living in an inpatient treatment setting has been *neglected, battered and/or sexually abused*. The next two chapters deal with this group of young clients.

Van Loon and Verhey point out that 40% of the children in the setting they work at (the Child and Adolescent Psychiatric Clinic of the Sophia Children's Hospital in Rotterdam) have been neglected or physically abused. They describe the broad spectrum of symptoms that can be observed in these children. Within that they single out four underlying sources of maladjustment: unfavourable characteristics of the child as a result of early deficits in the parent-child relationship; organic and/or constitutional disorders; inadequate coping mechanisms; and an unfavourable mix of various developmental aspects. At the same time the treatment course and the way in which it has developed, based on experiences at the Clinic, is outlined (in nine stages).

Pannekoek reports from three residential pedagogical treatment centres in the heart of the Netherlands on his findings regarding sexually abused adolescents. Twenty-three percent of the residents have been or are suspected to have been abused (38% of the girls, 11% of the boys). He shows how staff can deal with experiences or indications of abuse suggested by residents during the intake and the treatment stage. Here Pannekoek elaborates on the question of how 'to break through the silence', how to act in the living unit, and what all of this requires from the staff. The author advocates an advancement in know-how concerning the subject of sexual abuse.

For many young people in residential homes social incompetence is such an enormous handicap that, in several theories of residential treatment, this problem is considered to be one of the central points on which the child care process should be focused (e.g. Whittaker, 1979; Van der Ploeg, Van den Bergh, Klomp, Knorth & Smit, 1992). In the next two chapters the authors describe *specific types of programs* to strengthen the *social competence of residential youths*.

Keulen tells about a program for experiential learning. The HHK, a Dutch institution for residential care in The Hague has gained experience with this program over the last several years. It entails a three-month so-called 'Survival Trek' in Norway, in which six youths and two staff members participate. Characteristic of the youths is that they show serious forms of problem behaviour and have already been in a number of different institutions. Besides describing the program, the author presents some research results on about 50 youths, who have participated in a Trek over the last several years. The (positive) results are connected to six 'active' components in the program. At the same time Keulen makes a plea for more research.

Another project, described here by **Slot and Zandberg,** is the 'Working and Living Together' program (WLT) for deaf children with severe types of anti-social behaviour. It is a relatively new, still experimental project, in which a limited number of youths live communally on a farm with a resident counsellor and his family. Several trainers, teachers and supervisors are also engaged in the project. An important source of inspiration are the experiences acquired with so-called 'Kursushuizen', a Dutch adaptation of an American community-based program for anti-social youths called 'Achievement Place'. The three main components of this program (motivation system, teaching by instruction and modelling, and partial self-government) are used to build a competence-training program, designed for a special target group.

Besides devoting more attention to possibilities for strengthening the social competence of residential youths, we also find more and more descriptions of methods and experiments in which the *co-operation with the family or the parents* of children in care is a prominent theme. The next two chapters deal with this subject.

Verzaal goes into the method used in 'Op Dreef', a residential institution for court-ordered adolescent girls in Amsterdam. In this setting some important discoveries concerning co-operation with parents have been made over the last five years: (1) from the very first moment of contact parents should be involved in the assistance process; (2) the amount of time a girl stays in the institution can be drastically reduced; (3) generally speaking the care is more effective and enduring, because the problems between the girl and her parents are being dealt with more professionally. Besides stating the most important assumptions of the program, thoughts about the implications of the method for the staff and the organization are also offered.

Klomp reports on parts of a research project that he did in seven small-scale institutions for residential adolescent care, which in the Netherlands are getting more and more attention: the so-called

14

halfway homes. Because these centres are primarily aimed at guiding youngsters in a process towards independence and getting away from the home environment, it is sometimes believed that parents should be only marginally involved. Klomp shows that the opposite is true.

1.3 The staff and the system; management issues

In Part II of this book some of the issues related to *managing an institution* are presented. At stake is the way in which the staff in residential institutions functions, a crucial factor for the quality of the process of care (cf. Schaefer & Swanson, 1988; Hellinckx, Broekaert, Vanden Berge & Colton, 1991). More to the point the questions are: How can problems and tensions on the work floor be met, how can the professionalism of residential workers be promoted and how can the organization offer support for this?

At first **Durning** describes the course of a crisis in a children's home in a Parisian suburb. It is a case study (based on a qualitative analysis of data gathered through participatory observation), in which we see how factors such as insufficient education/training of social workers, obscure job descriptions of the staff, ineffective communication between the workers and inadequate management can lead to a crisis in an entire institutional system as a result of a seemingly simple occurrence: the children created some trouble and made a lot of noise while changing shoes for slippers in a small corridor before having dinner! Convinced that such crisis situations are not unique to the setting mentioned, the author pleads for international comparative research.

In the following chapter **Challender** outlines a number of characteristics of the work in the residential sector in England which increases the chances of job stress, burnout and a high turnover among staff. (His observations can easily be supported by research results from other countries; for the Netherlands e.g. Van der Ploeg, Brandjes, Nass & Defares [1985].) Moreover he points to the fact that working with comparatively young social workers, barely past adolescence themselves, requires extra attention. The author pleads for every residential setting to take a number of measures and to create provisions (a support structure), inside as well as outside, that support the social workers in exercising their profession.

In a sector where one can observe a definite development towards small-scale projects, Ward's entry is remarkable. He states that an important instrument for designing care in homes is often not used enough because the staff is afraid of it: operating in and with 'the large group'. After an analysis of the sources of resistance against working with large groups, Ward presents a number of advantages, dividing practical from therapeutic functions. He also deals with the way interaction patterns in other places in the organization (e.g. among staff members themselves or between staff and children), are recreated during 'large group' meetings. This can be used as a theme for conscious reflection.

The three preceding contributions all emphasize the need for training and supervision of residential workers. Edens reports on research into a training program, aimed at reinforcing staff member's skills for coping with individual and group situations which they perceive as difficult. The curriculum is meant to: (1) increase relevant knowledge, (2) increase the behavioral repertoire, and (3) stimulate a professional attitude. This last item includes three principles: 'to be directive' (working according to a plan), 'acceptance' (showing that you understand the youngsters and accept them as people), and 'reinforcement' (focusing on things juveniles do well). The author shows that after the program participants in the training course scored significantly better on both knowledge and behavioral tests than a control group. Professional behaviour related to the above-mentioned aspects of attitude (the ability to regulate, to be empathic and to stimulate) improved the most.

Visser's contribution contains the development of an instrument for establishing the climate in an institution. The 'tool' the author provides is based on the thesis that analysis of the social system is indispensable in assessing how an institution is functioning. The author states that four functions, namely 'goal development', 'utilization of energy', 'development of structure' and 'communication with the surroundings', have to be adequately realized for the residential institution to be appreciated as meaningful and helpful. It is important that workers as well as clients be asked whether or not - and how - the functions mentioned above are being realized. Visser shows an example of an actual application of the analysis model

16

derived from a consultation project in an institute for abused women and their children. It offers the institutional staff valuable directions for a reflection on the way the institution is functioning.

If a residential institution wants to determine the quality of its program in order to enlarge it, research data can be a valuable aid. A type of research that is explicitly aimed at such a goal is often paraded as 'program evaluation' (Patton, 1986). In the Netherlands an example of a rather large research project of this kind is the 'Project Proefpolders' (Bijl & Van den Bogaart, 1992), in which five large residential institutions took part for three years. Essential was renewing, i.e. improving, parts of the program, guided in part by research. Actually this kind of research is a special example of so-called 'social policy research'; a type of research that centres around the evaluation of policy or intervention programs.

A reflection on some theoretical and methodological developments in this type of research is the substance of **Van de Vall's** contribution. The author focuses on 'clinical program evaluation', and shows that there are fundamentally three methods of research and intervention: a. impact evaluation (major question: is the policy or intervention goal being met?); b. process evaluation (with the question: how does the program run and which elements are responsible for a less than optimal impact?); and c. formative evaluation (major question: what recommendations can be made to improve the program?). Statements are made about the most important problems in each method and how these problems can be tackled.

References

Bijl, B., & Bogaart, P.H.M. van den (1992). Social climate and readiness for change. In J.D. van der Ploeg, P.M. van den Bergh, M. Klomp, E.J. Knorth, & M. Smit [eds.], *Vulnerable youth in residential care. Part I: social competence, social support and social climate*. Leuven: Garant.

Bryer, M. (1988). *Planning in child care*. London: BAAF.

Colton, M.J., & Hellinckx, W. [eds.] (1992). *Child care in the EC. Foster and residential care in the countries of the European Community*.

Aldershot: Avebury.

Harinck, F.J.H., & Smit, M. (1992, November). *Process evaluation in residential care*. Paper presented at the 2nd EUSARF Seminar 'Caring for troubled children: Current research on residential care, foster care and their alternatives', Paris.

Hellinckx, W., Broekaert, E., Vanden Berge, A., & Colton, M. [eds.] (1991). *Innovations in residential care*. Leuven: Acco.

Klomp, M., & Oeffelt, P.W.H.M. van (1978). Residentiële behandelingsplanning als proces. *Pedagogisch Tijdschrift, 3*, 387-404.

Knorth, E.J., & Smit, M. [eds.] (1990). *Residentiële jeugdhulpverlening; mogelijkheden voor planmatig werken*. Leuven/Apeldoorn: Garant.

Lyman, R.D., Prentice-Dunn, S., Wilson, D.R., & Taylor, G.E. (1989). Issues in residential and inpatient treatment. In R.D. Lyman, S. Prentice-Dunn, & S. Gabel [eds.], *Residential and inpatient treatment of children and adolescents* (pp. 3-22). New York / London: Plenum Press.

Patton, M.Q. (1986). *Utilization focused evaluation*. London: Sage Publications.

Ploeg, J.D. van der, Brandjes, M., Nass, C.H.T., & Defares, P.B. (1985). Stress bij groepsleiding. In J.D. van der Ploeg [ed.], *Jeugd (z)onder dak II* (pp. 46-61). Alphen aan den Rijn: Samsom.

Ploeg, J.D. van der, Bergh, P.M. van den, Klomp, M., Knorth, E.J., & Smit, M. [eds.] (1992). *Vulnerable youth in residential care. Part 1: social competence, social support and social climate*. Leuven: Garant.

Schaefer, C.E., & Swanson, A.J. [eds.] (1988). *Children in residential care; critical issues in treatment*. New York: Van Nostrand Reinhold.

Whittaker, J.K. (1979). *Caring for troubled children; residential treatment in a community context*. San Francisco: Jossey-Bass.

2 Four Features of Child Psychopathology An Interdisciplinary Model of Classification and Treatment

P.L.M. van der Doef

2.1 Introduction

In the following the relationship between the classification and treatment of childhood disorders is discussed on the basis of some core elements of two present-day psychiatric classification systems: the ICD (the International Classification of Diseases of the World Health Organization) and the DSM (the Diagnostic and Statistical Manual of the American Psychiatric Association). In a previous study (Van der Doef, 1988) a model of these elements was proposed, in which the problems of children were related to their intentional and adaptive dysfunctioning. This relationship is of a psychobiological nature. Intentionality is a psychological concept indicating the cognitive and emotional involvement of children with their environment (Calon & Prick, 1962). Adaptation is a biological concept referring, according to the theory of Piaget, to an equilibrium of exchange between the child and its environment (Ginsburg & Opper, 1969). For the treatment of children a separate model was proposed, in which the treatment was interpreted in terms of mathematical game theory. This theory focuses on problems of cooperation in social interactions (Axelrod, 1984). However, the existence of two separate models for the classification and treatment of childhood disorders is unsatisfactory since the treatment of children somehow has to be related to the psychopathological disturbances of the children and their classification. So, the question is whether an integration between the two models is possible or not. Is it possible to relate a model of treatment to a model of the classification of childhood disorders?

In this paper this question is answered by proposing an integrated, interdisciplinary, model consisting of some core elements of the disciplines of psychiatry, psychology, pedagogy and biology. Each discipline, it is argued, represents its own specific information, which taken together makes an interdisciplinary model of classification and treatment possible. The discipline of psychiatry makes clear how childhood disorders are to be classified. The discipline of psychology gives an interpretation of this classification in terms of the psychological inner world of children. The discipline of pedagogy stresses the external pedagogical environment of the children, the way this environment provides a basis for treatment. Lastly, the discipline of biology specifies the process of adaptation related to the childhood disorders.

The new model is based on the epistemological model presented by the French philosopher Michel Foucault (1966). This is the so-called 'quadrilateral of language' by means of which Foucault discusses the structure of the social sciences in several periods of history since the sixteenth century. Foucault's analysis of science basically is a linguistic exercise: he emphasizes the words in which the things are caught. His structure of science, therefore, is not limited to science, but is applicable, as we will specify for the treatment of childhood disorders, to any social process in which language plays a fundamental role.

2.2   Classification

In psychiatric classification systems of childhood disorders the following features are of central importance (Quay, 1986; Van der Doef, 1988; Veerman, 1990; Vandereycken, Hoogduin en Emmelkamp, 1990):
1) Autism or Pervasive Developmental Disorders;
2) Attention Deficit Disorders;
3) Anxiety Disorders;
4) Conduct Disorders.
Comparison of the differences and similarities of these four features in a previous study (Van der Doef, 1988) revealed the model of figure 1.

Intentionality	Adaptation	
	Assimilation	Accommodation
Cognition	Autism	Attention Deficit Disorder
Emotion	Anxiety Disorder	Conduct Disorder

Figure 1   A biopsychological interpretation of childhood disorders

In the model of figure 1, psychopathological disorders of childhood are related to the psychological function of intentionality and the biological function of adaptation. Both intentionality and adaptation are divided into two complementary parts or aspects. Intentionality is divided into cognition and emotion. This division is familiar in both the earlier phenomenological tradition in The Netherlands (Calon & Prick, 1962) and the more recent international tradition of computational technology and cognitive psychology (Oatley, 1987; Williams, Watts, MacLeod & Mathews, 1991). Adaptation is divided into assimilation and accommodation according to the theory of Jean Piaget (Ginsburg & Opper, 1969). In this theory the process of accommodation describes the individual's tendency to change in response to environmental demands. The process of assimilation is the complementary process by which the individual incorporates elements of the external world into his current psychic structures.

Autism is related to cognition and assimilation because of the problems of autistic children in exploring a new environment (assimilation). These difficulties are a result of cognitive inabilities (Van Engeland, 1990). The organization of the behaviour of autistic children is rigid and ritualistic. They are not able to incorporate new environmental elements into their cognitive structures. Because of the complementary nature of the processes of assimilation and accommodation, problems of assimilation have their impact on the process of accommodation. So we should not be surprised to see autistic children also showing problems of accommodation, i.e. they do not change easily in response to environmental demands. Prominent in the syndrome of autism, however, is the rigid cognitive structure of these children preventing them from incorporating elements of the external world.

Prominent in the syndrome of attention deficit disorder (ADD), on the other hand, is the inability of these children to change in response to environmental demands (accommodation). ADD children lack a sufficient amount of continuous selective attention, they cannot inhibit impulses and/or are physically underaroused (Verhulst, 1990). The cognitive basis of these problems often cannot be easily separated from the emotional basis of the difficulties that children with conduct disorders (CD) show with respect to environmental demands. So, attention deficit disorders and conduct disorders are closely related syndromes (two types of accommodation problems in terms of figure 1), which are often discussed in relation to each other (Werry, 1986 a, b; Taylor, 1988; Verhulst, 1990).

Anxiety disorders and conduct disorders are regarded to be of an emotional nature. Anxious children do not easily assimilate new environments, they show emotional problems when they have to function in separation from their parents - just as their parents often do, the other side of the symbiotic educational coin. According to the DSM-III-R at least three types of anxiety may be discerned: excessive anxiety concerning separation from those to whom the child is attached (separation anxiety), excessive shrinking from contact with unfamiliar people (avoidant disorder) and an excessive or unrealistic anxiety or worry (overanxious disorder).

Children with a conduct disorder are breaking societal rules; they steal, run away, lie, set fire, destroy, fight, etc. These are all behaviours contradictory to environmental educational demands, which is the accommodation side of adaptation in terms of Piaget. In children with conduct disorders, cognitive deficits may be present, but the emotional refusal to obey to environmental rules stands on the foreground. In the words of John Werry (1986b, p. 9) is it hard to escape the impression that ADD (Attention Deficit Disordered) children are viewed as sick and/or not responsible for their problems, while CD (Conduct Disordered) children are viewed as bad. According to Werry this is well reflected in the way these two disorders are handled: ADD is seen primarily by the helping systems while CD tends to be relegated to the law enforcement systems.

2.3 Interdisciplinary structure of treatment

In this section the above discussed four basic psychiatric disorders of childhood are projected into a new model, the epistemological model proposed by Michel Foucault (1966). This model consists of four elements, which are clockwise arranged in a quadrilateral such as figure 2. All four elements are compared with each other and the resulting resemblances and differences are noted in the space outside the quadrilateral. The two crossing spaces, from which the quadrilateral arises, may be thought of as a field of knowledge. Foucault speaks of an epistemological field.

In figure 2 the model is filled in with the four discussed categories and the two epistemological fields of psychology and pedagogy. These two fields may be conceived of as an inner psychological space and an outer pedagogical space. The transition between these two fields is named in biological terms, in terms of adaptation or the equilibrium of exchange between the individual and his environment.

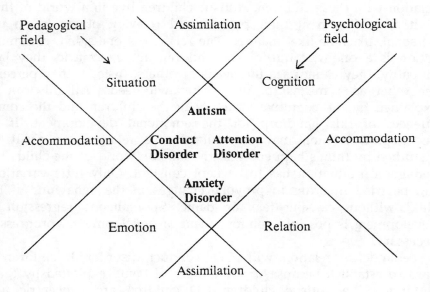

Figure 2   *An interdisciplinary model of the classification and treatment of childhood disorders*

The relationship between the psychiatric and the psychological categories corresponds to the model of figure 1. Autism and attention deficit disorder are seen as cognitive problems, conduct disorders and anxiety disorders as emotional problems. The adaptational specification is mentioned in between the psychological and the pedagogical fields. This place marks the transition between an internal psychological world and an external pedagogical environment. Autism and anxiety disorders are related to assimilation, to problems of incorporating a new environment into a psychic structure. Attention deficit disorders and conduct disorders are related to accommodation, to problems of changing in response to environmental demands.

The pedagogical field is divided into the complementary parts of situation and relation. This division is owed to Stellwag (1970), who discusses the fundamental importance for the pedagogical science of these two basic categories. The relationship between the psychiatric and the pedagogical categories may be conceptualized as follows.

In autism and conduct disorder a situational source of treatment is indicated because of the difficulties in establishing an pedagogical relation with these children. Autistic children live in a world of their own and often treat their parents and relevant others in an unpersonal, machine-like, manner. The relation is one-sided, communication is a one-way traffic. The children are egocentric, they lack empathy, they cannot see the needs of others. Instead, they perceive the other as a means to fulfil their own needs. All this can be explained by the cognitive structure of the children and the consequences of this handicap for the emotional development. If an pedagogical relation may be realized, this relation can easily be disturbed by things happening in the outside world of the child. The pedagogical situation has to be kept constant. Only little variations can be tried in order to provoke changes in the behaviour of the child without causing fear or panic. Spontaneous regression in development is possible, reinforcement of developmental progress is necessary.

A pedagogical relation with CD (conduct disordered) children is hard to establish because of the danger of being exploited by these children. Like autistic children CD children are egocentric and perceive the other primarily as a threat or as a means to fulfil their needs. Unlike autistic children, CD children are primarily disturbed in their emotions and one may be tempted to base a treatment on an emotional relationship with these children. Often then, one is deceived when the child is out of sight of the educator. Out of sight, out of mind. If not controlled by situational demands, the children follow the voice of their frustrated impulses and try to catch what they can get. For the treatment of these children it is essential to replace an external control of the situation with an internal control of the situation. Responsibility is the key-word of treatment. The pedagogical situation is a rich source of practising responsibility. Children may be stimulated to learn how to manage their own money, food, furniture, clothing, leisure-time, etc.

For children with attention deficit and anxiety disorders the model stresses the pedagogical relation as a primary source of treatment. Stressing this relation does not mean that a situational source is not to be used. Especially children with attention deficit disorders (ADD) need a structured situation. This condition being satisfied, however, with ADD children an open pedagogical relation is possible. This is in contrast to CD (conduct disordered) children with whom such an open relation often is not possible. When the vicious circle of unstructured behaviour, negative reactions and a negative self-image is broken, the ADD child is in a position to make up a social arrear and to restore the pedagogical relation with its parents.

For children with anxiety disorders the pedagogical relation is a means of reducing anxiety, loosening the symbiotic attachment to the parents and helping them to learn social skills. In the pedagogical relation security is given. By being together with the parent, the child learns the social meanings of behaviour (Spiecker, 1984). There are two sides to this relationship: the parent can be a good, as well as a bad model. The child may learn not only constructive meanings, but also destructive ones. The latter meanings have to be corrected, if possible, in treatment. In treatment constructive educational meanings may be offered to the child and its family.

2.4   Conclusion

We want to conclude the above presentation of the model with a few remarks. The model provides, it is argued, a coherent view on a social practice, in our case the treatment of childhood disorders in

26

relation to their classification. According to the model the treatment of childhood disorders consists of helping children to find a balance with their environment in terms of cognition and emotion, of assimilation and accommodation and of the pedagogical relation and situation. This balance is absent or disturbed. How a balance actually has to be found or restored in the course of treatment is a complicated story falling outside the scope of this paper and remaining to be told in future work. In the above presentation only some main features of classification and treatment could be discussed which can be further elaborated. The presented model clearly shows that a meaningful relationship between the classification and treatment of childhood disorders can be constructed and that knowledge from several disciplines can be integrated into an interdisciplinary model.

References

Axelrod, R. (1984). *The evolution of cooperation.* New York: Basic Books.
Calon, P.J.A., & Prick, J.J.G. (1962). *Psychologische grondbegrippen.* Arnhem: Van Loghum Slaterus.
Doef, P.L.M. van der (1988). *De orthopedagogische betekenis van problematisch kindgedrag.* Amersfoort/Leuven: Acco.
Engeland, H. van (1990). Autisme en psychosen. In W. Vander eycken, C.A.L. Hoogduin, & P.M.G. Emmelkamp [eds.], *Handboek psychopathologie, deel 1* (pp. 383-401). Houten/Antwerpen: Bohn Stafleu Van Loghum.
Foucault, M. (1966). *De woorden en de dingen.* Baarn: Ambo.
Ginsburg, H., & Opper, S. (1969). *Piaget's theory of intellectual development.* Englewood Cliffs: Prentice-Hall.
Oatley, K. (1987). Cognitive science and the understanding of emotions. *Cognition and Emotion, 1,* 3 (special issue).
Quay, H.C. (1986). Classification. In H.C. Quay & J.S. Werry [eds.], *Psychopathological disorders of childhood.* New York: John Wiley.
Spiecker, B. (1984). De pedagogische relatie. In B. Spiecker, B. Levering & A.J. Beekman [eds.], *Theoretische pedagogiek* (pp. 97-114). Meppel: Boom
Stellwag, H.W.F. (1970). *Situatie en relatie.* Groningen: Wolters-Noord-

hoff.

Taylor, E.A. (1988). Attention deficit and conduct disorder syndromes. In M. Rutter, A.H. Tuma & J.S. Lann [eds.], *Assessment and diagnosis in child psychopathology* (pp. 377-407). New York: Guilford Press.

Vandereycken, W., Hoogduin, C.A.L., & Emmelkamp, P.M.G. [eds.] (1990). *Handboek psychopathologie, deel 1.* Houten/Antwerpen: Bohn Stafleu Van Loghum.

Veerman, J.W. (1990). *De ontwikkeling van kinderen na een periode van klinische jeugdhulpverlening.* Amersfoort/Leuven: Acco.

Verhulst, F.C. (1990). Aandachts- en gedragsstoornissen. In W. Vandereycken, C.A.L. Hoogduin, & P.M.G. Emmelkamp [eds.], *Handboek psychopathologie, deel 1* (pp. 402-421). Houten/Antwerpen: Bohn Stafleu Van Loghum.

Werry, J.S. (1986a). Attention deficit, conduct, oppositional disorders I. *Journal of the American Academy of Child Psychiatry.*

Werry, J.S. (1986b). Differential diagnosis of attention deficits and conduct disorders. In L. Bloomingdale [ed.], *Attention Deficit Disorder, vol. IV.* New York: Spectrum.

Williams, J.M.G., Watts, F.N., MacLeod, C., & Mathews, A. (1990). *Cognitive psychology and emotional disorders.* New York: Wiley.

3   Juveniles Difficult to Place

P.H. van der Laan

3.1   Introduction

On December 31st 1990, 17,307 Dutch children and youngsters under the age of 18 were placed under a measure of child protection (Junger-Tas, Kruissink & Van der Laan, 1992).[1] 11,958 of them were placed under a supervision order.[2] In the Netherlands, a supervision order is taken when children are 'threatened with moral or physical danger', as the law puts it. A family guardian is appointed by the juvenile judge, to assist and advice the parents in the upbringing and education of their child (Junger-Tas, 1984). Originally, when the measure was introduced in the 1920's, a child under a supervision order was not to be removed from home. The measure was meant as an alternative to removal from home. With the help of the family guardian conditions should be created so that the child could stay at home (Doek, 1972). However, today more than half of all children and young people under a supervision order is living in institutions, foster families, or on their own.

Of those 11,958 children and young people under a supervision order, 6,489 are 12 to 17 years of age; 55% boys and 45% girls. In this age-category, only one third is staying at home with their parents. Two thirds are placed in residential or foster care, or living on their own.

---

[1] Dutch population (0-17 years) 3,298,000.

[2] Other measures being release and removal of parental rights, for various reasons both considered to be more intervening, more severe than a supervision order.

Here, we will concentrate ourselves on the group of juveniles, aged 12 to 17, in residential care. And more in particular on those, who have been placed frequently in residential care in a relatively short period of time. Also, most of those juveniles have a history of many unsuccessful attempts to be admitted into residential care. It seems as if residential care fails to provide these youngsters with the care they need. They lack the social support necessary to cope with their problematic situation. These are the juveniles, who are considered, by juvenile judges and family guardians, as 'difficult to place'.

3.2 Concern among juvenile judges

The concept 'difficult to place' is a complex one. In 1988, the Dutch association of juvenile judges asked the Research and Documentation Centre of the Ministry of Justice to pay attention, by means of research, to their problems with specific juveniles. It seemed as if it was primarily a problem of capacity. Juvenile judges found themselves confronted continuously with large numbers of juveniles, who were repeatedly running away from institutions (Van Teeffelen, 1990). A shortage of capacity in secure or semi-secure accommodation - the only type of institution capable to keep juveniles 'inside' - seemed to them to be the main problem. But running-away, in their opinion, had also, to some extent, to do with long waiting-lists in institutions for highly intensive treatment. Groups of juveniles who cannot be placed in institutions for intensive treatment, are placed in institutions with a less intensive type of treatment. These institutions, however, are unable to deal with these difficult youngsters. Running-away being the result. Therefore, a shortage of capacity of institutions for highly intensive treatment was definitely part of the problem.
Research should provide them with the necessary data that would put them in the right. Data that would enable them to convince the Ministry of Justice to put up more secure and semi-secure accommo-

dations and also more institutions for highly intensive treatment.[1]

3.3 Juveniles under supervision in residential care

To get a first impression of the extent of the problem, we took a closer look at all judicial[2] admissions in residential care of 12 to 17-year-olds during the second half of 1988 (Van der Laan, 1990).
During the second half of 1988 1,256 actual admissions had taken place. We were able to collect data on 807 of them (64%), which involved 717 juveniles.[3]
It is important to note, that more than 80% of these admissions took place in the intended institutions; that is to say, the institutions the authorities had in mind when they decided to refer the juvenile to residential care. Thus, a large majority of the juveniles were placed in the institutions, which were considered appropriate to meet their needs. Almost 75% of these placements were accomplished within a reasonable period of time, according to the authorities in charge of placing. Where this was not the case, other institutions were approached as an alternative in about half of all cases, without success however. The younger the juveniles, the more attempts were made.
Almost 20% of all placements did not take place in the intended institutions. The main reason, in two thirds of these cases, being that no place was available in the institution chosen. In almost 15% of the cases the institution chosen turned out to be an inappropriate treat-ment-setting. For instance, because of the fact that the institution chosen does not offer the kind of help needed. In many of these cases other institutions were tried (on average 2.4 attempts to place elsewhere).
Quite a remarkable outcome has to do with the type of institution

---

[1] Frankly, we did not think that the problem of 'juveniles difficult to place' would be that simple. There should be more than just a problem of running away, or just a shortage of capacity.
[2] That is to say, placements by juvenile judges, by Councils of Child Care and Protection, and by societies for guardianship.
[3] During that period 639 youngsters were placed only once, 66 juveniles were placed twice, 11 juveniles three times, and 1 boy four times.

Quite a remarkable outcome has to do with the type of institution where juveniles were placed. There were not only juveniles being placed in less severe institutions than felt necessary, but also the other way around: juveniles being placed in more severe types of institutions than needed.

On average 75 days passed between the decision to place a juvenile in an institution and the actual admission. In case of admission in an institution for intensive treatment, on average 120 days had passed.

Not surprisingly, juveniles are being placed in institutions for various reasons. They are mentioned in table 1.

Table 1   *Reasons for referring juveniles to residential care (in %; n=807)**

reason	%
behaviourial problems at home	49.2
pedagogical impotence of parents	38.8
relational problems between parents and child	32.1
running away/wandering	27.4
delinquency (not serious: vandalism, simple theft)	21.7
behaviourial problems at school	21.1
problems in preceding setting	19.6
learning problems/truancy	11.2
relational problems between parents	9.3
psychiatric problems	8.8
parental neglect	7.9
sexual abuse	7.6
alcohol and drug abuse	6.3
delinquency (serious: violence, serious property crime)	4.6
child-abuse	3.0
other	25.6

* Juveniles can be referred for more than one reason. Therefore, percentages add up to over 100%.

These results left us with the impression, that the concept of 'juveniles difficult to place' has partly to do with a shortage of capacity of specific treatment oriented institutions, and along with that with waiting-lists, partly with specific problematic backgrounds of the juveniles concerned, and partly with the dynamics of referring juveniles to care and admitting them into care.

This would mean that some of the problems may be overcome by increasing the capacity of specific institutions. Other problems cannot be overcome this way, since they have to do with shortcomings in knowledge and information about residential care, about specific institutions and what kind of help they offer, and about the problematic backgrounds of the juveniles and the kind of help they need.

3.4 Juveniles difficult to place

Sofar, we had gained only some general idea of what was going on. More specific, more detailed information was needed. For that reason, juvenile judges in 6 out of 19 court-districts were asked to select, on the 1st of January 1990, all juveniles under a supervision order they considered 'difficult to place' (Van der Laan, Verwers & Essers, 1992).[1]

They selected 359 juveniles, almost 25% of all juveniles under supervision and not staying at home. Their files were consulted to sort out the individual admission histories. Next, the family guardians were interviewed in order to complete the admission histories and to get more detailed information on the problematic backgrounds of their pupils. About 90% of the family guardians agreed with the juveniles judges as far as the judgement 'difficult to place' was concerned. In 10% of the cases they disagreed, but they missed other pupils on the list; they would have selected some others. So, all in all the total number would have been the same.

The juveniles selected as 'difficult to place' differ from the total population of juveniles under a supervision order in residential care on a number of characteristics.[2]

---

[1] We decided not to do the selection ourselves, since we did not want to impose our own criteria of what should be considered 'difficult to place', on the juvenile judges. They had asked for attention to this phenomenon, and we did not want them, afterwards, to disagree with the selection of youngsters examined.

[2] Data on the total population correspond with those of Vissers (1989) and Van der Ploeg & Scholte (1988).

Firstly, the period of time they are under supervision, is much shorter; on average 10.3 months against 31.6 months for the population as a whole.

Secondly, during the period they are under a supervision order, they are placed in an institution almost twice as many times; on average 4.6 times against 2.8 times. The same applies to the number of unsuccessful attempts to have them admitted: 4.7 times against 2.4 times. With regard to the period of time under supervision, 'juveniles difficult to place' are placed in an institution once every 7 months, other juveniles under a supervision order once every 14.6 months.

On average they are a little older: more 16 and 17-year-olds among 'juveniles difficult to place'. The number of girls is slightly under-represented : 35% against 45% in the total population. Youngsters from ethnic minorities, in particular Surinamese and Moroccan boys, are overrepresented: 40% against 20 to 25%.

They also differ with respect to their problematic background, as table 2 shows.

Table 2   *Reasons for referring juveniles to residential care (in %)**

reason	juveniles difficult to place (n=359)	juveniles under supervision (n=807)
pedagogical impotence of parents	83.0	38.8
relational problems between parents and child	82.2	32.1
behaviourial problems at home	73.7	49.2
behaviourial problems at school	58.0	21.1
learning problems/truancy	43.7	11.2
running away/wandering	43.1	27.4
delinquency (not serious: vandalism, simple theft)	39.0	21.7
parental neglect	30.0	7.9
psychiatric problems	23.7	8.8
alcohol and drug abuse	17.2	6.3
delinquency (serious: violence, serious property crime)	16.3	4.6
child-abuse	13.7	3.0
sexual abuse	11.8	7.6

* Juveniles can be referred for more than one reason. Therefore, percentage add up to over 100%.

As far as personal characteristics are concerned, there is little doubt that 'juveniles difficult to place' differ from the general population of juveniles under a supervision order. As a group they show far more problems, and many of the problems seem to be more serious.[1] Both groups differ from each other significantly.

Furthermore, they have been placed in institutions more frequently in a shorter period of time, and also that more attempts are made to have them admitted in institutions.

3.5 Admission history

Table 3 gives an overview of types of institutions (including foster care), where juveniles have been placed and where attempts have been made.

Table 3   *Admissions/attempts and type of institution (in %)*

type of institution	admissions (n=1614)	attempts (n=1429)
institution for intensive treatment	7.1	17.8
reception home (private)	8.9	4.2
institution for treatment (state)	3.0	3.9
reception home (state)	10.3	3.4
mental hospital	1.9	5.9
institution for treatment	13.9	25.1
vocational training institution	5.3	11.7
home for mentally retarded children	4.4	8.3
crisis intervention	18.8	4.3
institutions for normal children	16.9	14.3
foster families	9.4	0.1

Quite many placements (almost 40%) have taken place in reception

---

[1] In table 2, for 'juveniles difficult to place' we have only included problems, of which family guardians were convinced that they apllied to their pupils to a high degree. These are problems, they marked as 4 or 5 on a 5-point scale, ranging, from not-present to very-much-present. In case we should have included problems rated 2 or 3 (slightly and moderately present) as well, the difference between the two groups would have been even bigger.

homes and institutions for crisis intervention. Reception homes operated by the state or privately operated, are secure accommodation. Since this type of institution, in general, is capable more easily to provide room on short notice, it illustrates that in many cases placing a juvenile in an institution is an urgent matter.

One quarter of all admissions is accomplished in treatment homes (institutions for intensive treatment, state treatment homes, and 'normal' treatment homes).

As far as attempts are concerned, a different picture appears. Almost half of all attempts concerns treatment facilities. Far less attempts are made to place in reception homes (10%).

Girls are, relatively, more frequently placed in institutions for intensive treatment than boys are. The same applies to attempts. This has partly to do with the relatively small variety of types of institutions available to girls. For instance, almost all vocational training institutions are for boys exclusively.

Furthermore, attempts to place in institutions for intensive treatments outnumber placements. No doubt that this illustrates a shortage of capacity in this type of institutions.

Juveniles stay in an institution for approximately 5 months, but this may vary according to the type of institution (see table 4).

Table 4   *Length of stay*

type of institution	average number of months
institution for intensive treatment	7.1
reception home (private)	2.4
institution for treatment (state)	6.6
reception home (state)	2.3
mental hospital	4.5
institution for treatment	7.1
vocational training institution	8.1
home for mentally retarded children	9.7
crisis intervention	1.5
institutions for normal children	6.6
foster families	5.2

The average length of stay in reception homes is relatively short. This, of course, has to do with the admission having only a temporary character The period of time spent in treatment homes or institutions with vocational training facilities, however, is not much longer. One may doubt whether this allows us to speak of actual treatment or training.

3.6 Terminated placements

Reasons for terminating residence may explain why this group of youngsters spend, on average, such a short time in specific types of institution. Together with the reasons for attempts being unsuccessful, they may give us insight why these juveniles are considered 'difficult to place' (see table 5).

Table 5   *Reasons for terminating residence (in %)**

reason	%
temporary stay **	26.7
juvenile ran away	22.8
juvenile is sent away	22.3
penal placement terminated	8.6
divergence between care offered and problems of juvenile	8.3
temporary admission, meant for observation	5.1
juvenile is not motivated	4.9
juvenile showed positive development	3.5
juvenile back home (in positive sense)	3.3
temporary (penal/correction) placement	1.5
institution does not link with religious background juvenile	0.9
internal problems in institution	0.9
juvenile has become of age	0.8
age (too old; too young)	0.6
juvenile back home (in negative sense)	0.4
other	2.3
unknown	4.8

* Residential care can be terminated for more than one reason. Therefore, percentages add up to over 100%.
** Until room is available in other institution

A group of 348 juveniles [1] accounted for 1,614 admissions. 1,383 of them were terminated at one moment. In table 5 the reasons for this are listed. (There can be more than one reason for terminating a stay in residential care.)

Over 46% of all placements are terminated because of negative reasons; running away and sending away (the institution not capable to cope with the behaviourial problems of the juvenile) being mentioned quite frequently. Only 7% of all placements are terminated for positive reasons. The reason most frequently mentioned (temporary stay while waiting for room in another institution) tells us something about shortage of capacity, waiting-lists etcetera.

Some of the reasons are related more specificly to certain types of institutions than other. A temporary stay, for instance, is closely related to reception homes and crisis intervention, and running away to treatment homes and institutions with vocational training facilities. And, finally, sending away is related to homes for mentally retarded children and, again, treatment homes and vocational training institutions.

Data are available on 1,419 unsuccessful attempts to have juveniles admitted in residential care.[2] Table 6 lists the reasons for attempts being unsuccessful.

More than one of every attempt is unsuccessful, just because no room is available. In one quarter of all cases, juveniles are not admitted, because the institution chosen does not offer the assistance and help needed.

Needless to say, some of the reasons for attempts being unsuccessful are quite strongly related to specific types of facilities. Especially treatment facilities, and more in particular institutions for highly intensive treatment, have to refuse admittance frequently; in up to 70% of all referrals, just because there is no room available.

---

[1] 11 juveniles were not actually placed, despite the fact that their family guardians and juvenile judges took efforts to place them in an institution.

[2] 58 juveniles had only admissions on their records and no attempts.

Table 6   *Reasons for attempts being unsuccessful (in %)**

reason	%
divergence between care offered and problems of juvenile	25.6
no room available, juvenile on waiting-list	23.7
no room available, immediate refusal	13.9
lack of motivation juvenile	10.6
proceedings stayed, juvenile placed elsewhere/other solution found	9.5
intellectual level too high/low	4.0
juvenile does not show up	3.9
age (too old/young)	3.3
parents do not agree with institution chosen	2.5
institution does not link with intake procedure still on	1.7
religious background of juvenile	1.0
gender	0.4
other	2.3
unknown	12.3

* An attempt can be unsuccessful for more than one reason. Therefore, percentages add up to over 100%.

3.7   A complex concept

As is said earlier, the concept of 'juveniles difficult to place' is a complex one. There is a wide range of psycho-social problems, a wide range of reasons for unsuccessful attempts to place and for terminating a juvenile's residence. Therefore, it is definitely not only a matter of shortage of capacity, although it is an important factor. This is acknowledged by family guardians, when asked about factors causing 'juveniles difficult to place'. Table 7 contains factors, which have caused 'juveniles difficult to place', according to the family guardians concerned.

The factors are of a different character. Some have to do with shortage of capacity, some with a lack of variety of facilities, some with specific characteristics of the juveniles concerned, and some with the problematic backgrounds of the juveniles. Together they add to the problem, experienced by juvenile judges and family guardians.

Table 7   *Factors causing 'juveniles difficult to place' (in %)**

factor	%
psycho-social problems juvenile	84.9
waiting-time before admission	61.4
lack of motivation juvenile	58.6
proper care not available	57.5
running away	48.8
refusals because of lack of room	42.8
age	24.6
parents not co-operative	22.5
large number of transfers	18.2
gender	5.3
ethnic background	1.9

* More than one factor could be mentioned. Therefore, percentages add up to over 100%.

3.8   What should be done?

Solutions suggested by family guardians are mainly in terms of facilities. To deal with the problem of 'juveniles difficult to place', an increase of capacity and of variety of specific residential facilities is needed (see table 8).

Table 8   *Possible solutions as mentioned by family guardians (in %)*

solution	%
open treatment accommodation with specific training facilities on the premises	22.9
secure accommodation with specific training facilities on the premises	18.7
secure accommodation with psychiatric treatment facilities and specific training facilities on the premises	13.0
open treatment accommodation, external treatment facilities	10.6
open accommodation with psychiatric treatment facilities	8.8
institution far away from home	8.8
secure accommodation with psychiatric treatment facilities	8.4
open accommodation set-up for specific ethnic groups with specific treatment facilities on the premises	6.7

However, much more can be done, and much more should be done. Just working on an increase of capacity and on a greater variety, will not solve the problem.

Placements should be prepared more carefully. The following, sometimes rather rhetorical, questions seem to be relevant (see also Knorth, 1988; Van den Bergh, 1991). Do authorities in charge of placing know about all treatment facilities available in the country or in their region? Do they make the right choice and can they make the right choice? Or, are they provided with insufficient information about treatment facilities by the institutions concerned, and therefore are mistaken in their referral? Do they provide the accepting institution with the proper kind of information on the juvenile concerned, or do they keep behind certain kinds of information, which in their opinion might endanger the admission, and may cause the institution to make the wrong decision? We have reason to believe that the issues raised by these questions, and referred to earlier in this contribution as the dynamics of placing, do play an important, and with respect to our problem, a negative role. Thus, these topics should definitely be addressed.

Special attention should be paid to those juveniles running away frequently. A more intensive way of personal coaching, by both the authorities in charge of placing (family guardians) and the institutions, may prevent at least part of the running-away. In that respect more social support should be provided. Involving the parents or other people close to the juvenile, may also help.

Another issue concerns motivation. Do we really want juveniles to be motivated to accept treatment? Is such a presumption realistic? Probably not, a lack of motivation is to be considered characteristic for this field of work. These juveniles are placed under a measure of child protection by court. They are placed in residential care by court as well. Although this is done by means of a civil order, both juveniles and their families experience such orders as punishments. Such an experience does not add to motivation. We shall have to live with it. It should make us aware of the fact, that motivation is something we have to work on, as soon as a juvenile enters an institution. Motivation is not a condition, under which treatment can take place, but a goal towards treatment should be directed.

Finally, seeking solutions in residential care only, seems to be a little old-fashioned and narrow-minded. Why not try outreach and tracking programs as they are carried out in certain parts of the USA? Outreach and tracking means leaving juveniles at home, or at whatever place they are living, and assisting them in an ambulatory manner. A social worker is appointed, having a case-load of only 5 to 6 juveniles. The social worker keeps track of a juvenile for a period of a year. Keeping track means that they are in contact with the youngster every day of the week, of which three times face-to-face. The juveniles are supported in their daily life (school, work, leisure time activities, setting up, renewing, and maintaining contacts with parents, family, and friends, etc.). Such an approach may bring a residential career to a stop, and may bring about a form of social support, until then unknown to the juvenile.

References

Bergh, P.M. van den (1991). *Beslist geïnformeerd...? Opnamebesluitvorming in internaten voor jeugdhulpverlening.* Leuven/Apeldoorn: Garant.

Doek, J.E. (1972). *Vijftig jaar ondertoezichtstelling.* Zwolle: Tjeenk Willink.

Junger-Tas, J. (1984). Holland. In M.W. Klein (ed.), *Western systems of juvenile justice.* Beverly Hills: Sage.

Junger-Tas, J., Kruissink, M., & Laan, P.H. van der (1992). *Ontwikkeling van de jeugdcriminaliteit en de justitiële jeugdbescherming: periode 1980-1990.* Arnhem: Gouda Quint.

Knorth, E.J. (1988). Moeilijke plaatsbaarheid of plaatsingsmoeilijkheid? *Jeugdbescherming en Onderzoek*, nr.20, 9-25.

Laan, P.H. van der (1990). *Wel geplaatst, maar... Een eerste verkenning van het verschijnsel moeilijk plaatsbare jongeren en de daarmee samenhangende capaciteitsproblemen in de residentiële hulpverlening.* Den Haag: WODC.

Laan, P.H. van der, Verwers, C., & Essers, A.A.M. (1992). *Moeilijk plaatsbare jongeren.* Arnhem: Gouda Quint.

Ploeg, J.D. van der, & Scholte, E.M. (1988). *Tehuizen in beeld.* Leiden: Rijksuniversiteit, Vakgroep Orthopedagogiek/COJ.

Teeffelen, P.A.J.Th. van (1990). Onmachtige kinderrechter. *Familie- en Jeugdrecht*, 12, 11, 247-248.

Vissers, J. (1989). *De residentiële carrière van jongeren in de kinderbescherming*. Den Haag: CWOK.

4 Information about the Client

P.M. van den Bergh

4.1 Introduction

The beginning of a residential treatment programme is crucial for the success of the further developments in that process (Lennhoff, 1967; Schwarzenbach, 1968; Schouten, Hirsch & Blankstein, 1974; Knorth, 1987). This is especially true when we realize that in the Netherlands an average of four or five children per working hour stand at the threshold of this process (Knorth, Van Diest & Van den Bergh, 1987). This finding is even more impressive when we deal with the number of unrealized placements. Results of a research project from Knorth & Smit (1984) showed that 40% of the intake applications were unsuccessful.

Before placement in a residential institution, there have often been many problems in the situation of the youth which justifies a decision for outplacement from his own family. In such a situation we can speak of a process of outplacement. During this process, of which the intake procedure is a part, information exchange and relation building plays an important role (Knorth, Van den Bergh & Van der Ploeg, 1984).

This means that information will be exchanged among a number of people to investigate the possibilities for a new, radical form of assistance in a situation where parents are no longer able to raise the children effectively. The people in this outplacement process are members of the client system (youth and parents) and residential institutions.

The mediators (the placement institutions) are the link between both parties. They play a role in the outplacement process, because they handle the communication between the client system and the residential institutions.

The decision situation, in which clients and the care-givers are involved, is full of uncertainties because there is no scientific knowledge available to indicate what kind of intervention may produce the best results.

Some recent Dutch studies (De Bruyn, 1988; Koning, 1987; De Jong, 1987; Van Odenhoven, 1987; Span, 1986; Knorth, 1987) of decision - research in the field of youth care show that all the authors mention in their research that the decision-making process is unclear and that there are doubts about its quality. The authors speak of badly-defined, risky, dynamic and complex decision problems.

They say they want more insight into this matter. Their methods for coping with this desire for insight vary from a little literature research, to a careful description of the actual state of affairs to the implementation of a powerful, formal decision strategy.

Whatever form it takes, the decision *process* is the focus of interest. The authors differ in the manner in which they work out (and maximize) the decision process, but all of them emphasize the *need for available information*: information regarding the situation or problem about a decision that has been taken. This is a conditio sine qua non.

One of the main characteristics of the process model in the 'decision conflict theory' of Janis and Mann (1977) is the question - a question which the decision maker must ask himself repeatedly - is there enough good information available to make a decision? They focus on this question because decision research results show that people often ignore relevant information or refuse to accept more information (De Bruyn, 1987; Knorth, 1987; Van der Pligt, 1988).

Therefore a decision maker must provide himself with *relevant and sufficient information*; this seems to be a basic requirement for an adequate process. This conclusion is one of the main points in our empirical study.

Often it appears that the social workers doing the placement decide for themselves what kind of information will be sent. The information about the youth differs in a number of cases in content and quality. The written information varies from a one-page letter to a thick dossier. Often there is no *systematic gathering* of client data before people take a decision (see also Bastiaansen, 1976; Pohl, Wladimiroff & Remmerswaal, 1983; De Beer, Ruijs & Breemer ter Stege, 1983). That means that people take decisions based on insufficient information. And then we complain about the quality of the work in residential care!

4.2 Method

In this project we examine the information taken in advance by the social workers doing the placement. The placement institution sends in a dossier or report about the client. The information transfer is therefore written. These 'second hand' data form the basis for the intake decision.

The research project focused on: what kind of information was available, the content of that information and the perception of the information by the members of the intake team.

Our inquiry was carried out in three residential care units for boys and girls ranging in age from 8 to 18. We investigated 186 dossiers over nine months.

The written information for every youth discussed in the intake team of the residential centre is collected using the Questionnaire Information Dossier (QID; in Dutch: FIOD). The items in the QID are based on other research studies of 'youngsters with psycho-social problems' in the Netherlands (cf. Bastiaansen, 1976; Van der Ploeg, 1979; Van der Laan, 1983; Smit & Verhappen, 1984; Mesman Schultz, 1977, 1988, 1986). On the basis of these research findings we distinguish six clusters in the QID:

1. General information
2. Demographic information
3. Family information
4. School/work information
5. Treatment information
6. Problem information

The QID was filled in by the researcher.

The perception of the information by the members of the intake team is registered by the Sociometric Decision Schedule (SDS; in Dutch: SBS). This is a questionnaire, which can easily be filled in by the

members of the intake team before and after the intake meeting.
The analyses of the data was done by SPSSX.

4.3   Results

4.3.1 *Demographic data*
The 186 dossiers contain an equal number of boys and girls. They
range from 8 years and 9 months to 21 years and 6 months of age.
We divided the age of the intake group into four categories. 72% of
the research group was between 14 and 17 years old. That means
that three-quarters of the decision-making processes in the intake
procedure involve this group.
36 youth in the intake group are part of an ethnic minority. That
represents 19% of our research population. Half of the group is from
Surinam, a former Dutch colony.
Eighteen percent of the dossiers do not contain any information
regarding the kind of placement (voluntary/judicial). In the three
institutions more than half are placed on a voluntary basis. Then we
examine the youth between 14 and 17, which includes three-quarters
of our research group. It is possible that there are more voluntary
placements among this group. The Chi-square value (3.47, df 3, $p =$
.32, $n = 132$) shows that this is not true.
It is surprising that for 20% of the cases nothing is known about the
kind of placement at the time of intake.

4.3.2 *The completeness of the dossiers*
On the basis of the information on each cluster of the QID we determined what information was missing.
The missing data in the cluster are added and then divided by the
total number of variables per cluster. These scores are recorded and
this results in a relative score between 0 (no information) and 1
(maximum information).
While a maximum of 6 is possible - as tables 1 shows - the total
degree of completeness is 3.2.
There is a large body of information in the 'demographic' and
'problem' clusters, but the latter shows a relatively large standard
deviation. This implies that for a number of adolescents there is a lot
of information on these data, while for another group of adolescents

next to nothing is known about this cluster.
The following variables. dominate in factor 1: vandalism, arson, prob-
lems with authorities, drugs, theft, aggression and school- problems.
We interpret this as *manifest problematic behaviour.*

Table 1   *The average values of the clusters of 186 dossiers (the s.d.
is given in brackets)*

Cluster	Total
1. General information	.37 (.10)
2. Demographic information	.93 (.15)
3. Family information	.41 (.10)
4. School/work information	.42 (.13)
5. Treatment information	.31 (.17)
6. Problem information	.81 (.23)
Total information:	3.2

In most cases, the data from the other clusters, namely general data,
family data, school/work data and treatment data are 'unknown'.
In general we can conclude that almost half the relevant data are not
known. Most available information deals with the adolescent and his
problems; very little is known about his family, his school/work
situation and his previous treatment.

4.3.3 The problems of the young people
We also analyzed the problems of these young people. We made a
factor analysis of all variables, in order to establish underlying
dimensions in their problems.
The first explorative analysis employed the Maximum Likelihood
(ML) method. The communalities of a few variables were too small,
and these have been omitted in the following analysis. On the basis
of the Chi-square values, a 4, 5 or 6-factor solution was considered.
Then we used the Principle Component Analysis (PCA). The rotation
technique was Varimax. Finally, we opted for a 4-factor solution,
based on the interpretation of the content of the factors (see table 2).

50

Table 2   *Principle Component Analysis of the problems in 150 dossiers (loadings with an absolute value of .35 or higher are in italics)*

Variables	Factor 1	Factor 2	Factor 3	Factor 4
(explained variance:	14.5	8.9	8.5	7.5)
Vandalism	*.82*	.05	-.01	.00
Arson	*.75*	.10	-.12	-.05
Problems with authorities	*.60*	.26	-.00	-.15
Drugs	*.51*	.12	.26	-.27
Theft	*.51*	-.11	-.03	.15
Aggression	*.47*	-.15	-.05	.02
School problems	*.41*	.21	.06	.16
Placement youth assistance	*.36*	*.77*	.10	.09
Previous treatment	-.08	*.75*	.18	.06
Runaway	.23	*.45*	.03	-.29
Isolation problems	.03	.20	*.63*	.09
Contact disorders (Socially inhibited)	-.06	.21	*.49*	*.42*
Problems with one of the parents	-.09	.03	*.47*	-.07
Identity problems	-.02	.04	*.45*	-.08
Language problems	.07	*-.36*	*.45*	.04
Bereavement	.21	*-.41*	*.44*	.15
Physical complaints	.06	-.16	.20	*.66*
Psychosomatic symptoms	-.09	.22	-.19	*.57*
Depression	-.07	-.05	-.11	*.52*
Problems with new partner of parent	-.14	.04	-.09	*-.36*
Suicidal feelings	-.01	.02	-.25	.25

The following variables play a dominant role in the second factor: placement, youth assistance, previous treatment and running away. We called this *problematic previous assistance*.
Factor 3 shows the variables: isolating problems, contact disorders,

problems with one of the parents, identity problems and mourning problems. We characterize these as *inter- and intra-psychic problems*.

The variables in factor 4 refer to *psychosomatic problems* (physical complaints, psychosomatic symptoms, depression).

In general, we conclude that the subjects of our investigation can be typified by manifest problematic behaviour.

4.3.4 Relation of the factors with demographic variables

In the QID we distinguish four demographic variables: sex, age, ethnicity and kind of placement (voluntary or judicial).

With regard to sex we see: boys and girls differ significantly (T-value: -3.58) in factor 1 (manifest problematic behaviour). Boys have significantly more manifest problematic behaviour than girls.

On the basis of the standard deviations we divided the factor scores into three categories: 1=very problematic, 2= moderately problematic and 3=little problematic behaviour. 85% of the subjects are found in category 2 and 3. 15% can be regarded as very problematic. As we expected, significantly more boys than girls are found in category 1 (Procedure Breakdown, p= .0002).

With regard to age we have made two categories: under fifteen, and over fifteen. The only significant difference in these two categories appears in factor 2 (problematic previous assistance) (T-value: 2.24). This means that the older youngsters have had more problems with the social care system (in the past) than the youngsters 15 and under. There are no significant differences regarding ethnicity (autochthonous/allochthonous).

When we look at the kind of placement (voluntary/judicial) there are significant differences for factor 1 (T-value: 2.23) and factor 2 (T-value: 3.34). The young people who have been placed judicially have significantly more manifest behaviour problems and more problems with previous assistance.

In general, we can conclude that boys have more manifest behaviour problems than girls. This is also true for the young people who have been placed on a judicial basis.

Therefore we conclude that boys not only have more manifest behaviour problems than girls, but that these problems are more serious.

With regard to the previous assistance placement, we see that the older youngsters and the youngsters who have been placed on a judicial basis have more problems. The explanation is that as a result of their longer history of assistance, these youngsters have more problems.

4.3.5 Perception of the information [1]

We asked the members of the intake team if they had received any oral or written information about the youths. We also asked them how they evaluate this information in terms of 'good' or 'bad'. The questionnaire data from the members of the intake team are aggregated to the case level. This means that there are mean values per case. Tables 3 and table 4 show their answers to these questions.

Table 3   The extent of information as rated by the members of the intake team

The extent	n	%
Inadequate Information	22	14%
Tolerable information	112	73%
Adequate Information	19	12%
Total	153	100%

In 73% of the cases the members of the intake team rated the information 'tolerable,' while in 12% of the cases the information was rated 'good' (adequate). In 14% of the cases people considered themselves 'inadequately' informed.

Table 4 shows the ratings of the information received.

In 66% of the cases the quality of the information is perceived as 'tolerable' and in 12% as 'good'. In 22% of the cases the quality of the information is considered to be unsatisfactory.

The extent of information and the rating of its quality are significantly related (Pearson correlation: .19, p = .009). That means that when

---

[1] The perception of the information was examined in two residential institutions. In the third institution it was not possible to examine the members of the intake team, because in this institution there was no central intake meeting.

the members of the intake team 'feel' that the information is inadequate the quality of the information is rated 'intolerable'.

Table 4   Rating of the quality of the information by the members of the intake team

Rating	n	%
Inadequate Quality	33	22%
Tolerable Quality	101	66%
Adequate Quality	19	12%
Total	153	100%

When we combine the perception of the quality and quantity of the information (both variables are summarized and divided by two), we can see that 25% of the members were 'badly' informed. In 59% of the cases the information is perceived as 'tolerable' and in 16% 'adequate.'

This is an important moment in the decision making process. In one of every four cases discussed in the intake team the information is perceived to be 'inadequate' in quantitative and qualitative terms. Nevertheless the members take a decision in that case. The decision literature shows that people often take a decision even when they have no adequate information. A possible explanation of this phenomenon is that the intake procedure is perceived as so compelling by the members of the residential institution that people find themselves 'forced' to take a decision.

4.4 Discussion and Conclusions

From the reports we can conclude that the reporting is characterized by incompleteness and 'one-sidedness' (see also Packman, Randall & Jacques, 1986).
The information is incomplete with regards to the family situation, the school and/or work situation, and the previous treatment of the

youth. It is one-sided because it deals almost exclusively with the *description of behaviour symptoms*. The reports are primarily problem-oriented. That makes it difficult for the decision makers to estimate the client's *positive possibilities*.

About the rating of the information about the client we conclude the following:

The information is rated tolerable or good in three-quarters of the cases. In one of four cases the members of the intake team perceived the quality and quantity as 'inadequate'. Nevertheless people take a decision in the team. Why do they do so?

We conclude that the three institutions in our study have a low standard regarding the information they need. They have no clear insight into the client's functioning (including his problem behaviour) during the intake phase. Decisions are not grounded on clear information about the client.

It is possible that there is a certain amount of economic pressure to admit the youth to a residential institution. That means that the institutions accept the fact that they have insufficient information about the client. The decision making process is based on too little information which raises the question of the quality of the youth assistance.

The question is also why do institutions gather so little information or why do they accept such information? We think that there are two possibilities.

First of all that in the field of youth assistance we have no reliable and valid instrument to determine facts about a poorly functioning client system. That means that the members of the intake team must take decisions with subjective information, which is not systematically composed.

Though a certain kind of subjectivity is not entirely out of place, it is better for the quality of the work if there is a more systematic and standardized assessment of information during the intake procedure.

In the second place we think that routine and speed during the intake procedure take precedence over considerations about the contents of the assistance. We can understand some of these issues, but we think that those responsible for the care have a duty to get the maximum amount of information possible.

The information must be supplied and is not dependant on some social worker. Standardizing and having a system can be helpful in that case. That means that the receivers of the information deliver the written information about all the relevant aspects of the client and the client system.

Information about the youth should explicitly say what kind of goals are intended (cf. Van der Ploeg & Scholte, 1988). That makes it possible to look at the means for supporting these goals.

References

Bastiaansen, J.C.A. ((1976). *Het plaatsen van jeugdigen in tehuizen.* Roermond: POW Limburg.

Beer, G. de, Ruijs, H., & Breemer ter Stege, C (1983). *Er moet nou maar eens wat gebeuren.* Eindrapport van het onderzoek naar de wandelgang van minderjarigen door de jeugdhulpverlening in de regio Leiden/Aplhen aan den Rijn. Leiden: vakgroep Sociale Geneeskunde RUL.

Bergh, P.M. van den, Knorth, E.J., & Ploeg, J.D. van der (1985). Uithuisgeplaatst; communicatie en besluitvorming (II). Een tweede kwartet vragen na negen jaar onderzoek. *Tijdschrift voor Orthopedagogiek, 1,* 2-21.

Bergh, P.M. van den (1990). Cliëntinformatie van plaatsaanvragers. In E.J. Knorth & M. Smit (red.). *Residentiële jeugdhulpverlening. Mogelijkheden voor planmatig werken.* (87 - 98). Leuven/Apeldoorn: Garant.

Bergh, P.M. van den (1991). *Beslist Geïnformeerd ...?* Een onderzoek naar de opnamebesluitvorming in drie internaten voor jeugdhulpverlening. Leuven/Apeldoorn: Garant (dissertation).

Bruyn E.E.J. de (1987). Beslismomenten in de gedragswetenschappelijke hulpverlening. In J.D. van der Ploeg & P.M. van den Bergh (red.), *Besluitvorming en jeugdhulpverlening* (pp. 19-30). Leuven-/Amersfoort: Acco.

Bruyn, E.E.J. de (1988). Besluitvorming in de klinische psychodiagnostiek. *Nederlands Tijdschrift voor de Psychologie, 43,* 263-279.

Janis, I.L. & Mann, L. (1977). *Decision making. A psychological analysis of conflict, choice and commitment.* New York: Free Press.

Jong, A.J. de (1987). *Intake voor psychotherapie.* Meppel: Boom.

Knorth, E.J., & Smit M. (1984) Opname en uitval. In P.M. van den

Bergh, J.D. van der Ploeg & M. Smit (red.), *Grenzen van de residentiële hulpverlening* (pp. 40-69). Den Haag: VUGA.

Knorth, E.J., Bergh, P.M. van den, & Ploeg, J.D. van der (1984). Uithuisgeplaatst: kommunikatie en besluitvorming (I). Een eerste kwartet vragen na negen jaar onderzoek. *Tijdschrift voor Orthopedagogiek 12,* 559-578.

Knorth, E.J., Diest, C. van, & Bergh, P.M. van den (1987). Residentiële opname en besluitvorming. In J.D. van der Ploeg & P.M. van den Bergh (red.), *Besluitvorming en Jeugdhulpverlening* (pp. 71-88). Leuven/Amersfoort: Acco.

Knorth, E.J. (1987). *Opname op maat. Een verkennend onderzoek naar de intakeprocedure als begin van residentiële hulpverlening.* Leuven/Amersfoort: Acco.

Koning, R.F. *Wikken en Wegen een onderzoek naar intakeprocedures van psychotherapeutische gemeenschappen.* Noordwijkerhout: Stichting centrum St. Bavo (dissertation).

Laan, P.H. van der (1983). *Tehuisplaatsing van jongeren uit etnische minderheden.* Een onderzoek naar de problematiek rond de plaatsing in een tehuis of internaat van Surinaamse, Turkse en Marrokaanse jongeren. Den Haag: CWOK/Ministerie van Justitie.

Lennhoff, F.G. (1967). *Being sent away. The admission of children to residential settings.* Harmer Hill: Shotton Hall.

Mesman Schultz, K. (1977). *Aanpassing en predictie van aanpassing II.* Amsterdam SISWO.

Mesman Schultz, K. (1978). *De COM-procedure.* Een methode om voor de kinderbeschermingspupillen een advies te bepalen. Rijswijk: SISWO/CWOK.

Mesman Schultz, K., Depla, M., & Nelen, M. (1987). *Evaluatie van gedifferentieerde residentiële hulpverlening aan jeugdigen.* Leiden: LISBON (2e herziene druk).

Odenhoven, R. van *De opzet van de RIAGG-intake.* Utrecht: Nederlands Centrum Geestelijke Volksgezondheid (NcGV-reeks 104).

Packman, J., Randall, J., & Jacques, N. (1986). *Who needs care? Social work decisions about children.* Oxford: Basil Blackwell Ltd.

Pligt, J. van der (1988). psychologische Besliskunde. *Psychologie en Maatschappij, 45,* 327-339.

Ploeg, J.D. van der (1979). *Elfhonderd jeugdigen in tehuizen.* Utrecht: WIJN.

Ploeg, J.D. van der & Scholte, E.M. (188). *Tehuizen in beeld.* Leiden:

vakgroep orthopedagogiek/COJ.

Pohl, P.R.J., Wladimiroff, I., & Remmerswaal, P.W.M. (1983). *Plaatsingsadviescommissies, een beleidsadviserend verslag van vijf experimenten.* Nijmegen: Stichting GITP.

Schouten, J., Hirsch, S., & Blankstein, H. (1974). *Laat je niet kennen. Over residentiële behandeling van adolescenten.* Deventer: Van Loghum Slaterus.

Schwarzenbach, P. (1968). *Milieuwechsel. Am beispiel der Aufnahme von Kindern und Jugendlichen in Heime, Anstalten und Kliniken.* Bern: Huber (dissertation).

Smit, M. & Verhappen, J.M.J. (1984). *Jongeren tussen wal en schip. Interimrapport I.* Leiden: vakgroep Klinische en orthopedagogiek RUL.

Span, B. (1986). De rationaliteit van handhavings- en verwijzingsbeslissingen. In C.J.W. Meyer, S.J. Pijl & J. Rispens, *Beslissen over verwijzen en toelaten.* Lisse: Swets & Zeitlinger (RION: onderwijsonderzoek 2).

SPSSX (1983). *User's Guide SPSSX. New York: McGraw-Hill/SPSSX inc.*

Stein, T.J., & Rzepnicki, T.L. (1984). *Decision making in child welfare services. Intake and planning.* Boston/The Hague/Dordrecht/Lancaster: Kluwer-Nijhoff.

5   Residential Treatment of Maltreated Children

H. van Loon & F. Verheij

5.1   Introduction

What is child maltreatment? There is no overall consensus as to whether psychological maltreatment of a child includes parental behaviours involving physical or sexual contact with the child. One of the broadest conceptual definitions of psychological maltreatment was initially proposed by Garbarino, Guttman & Seeley (1986). For clinical practice it is important to stress that an act becomes psychological maltreatment to the extent that it is traumatic to the child. Emotional neglect and abuse are the end results of physical neglect and abuse. Johnson (1990) proposes a continuum to classify the various types of abuse. In this view, all forms of neglect and abuse are equated with psychological maltreatment. In this article we will use this definition.

The core problem of neglected and/or abused children is not merely a deficiency or a missing process with the child as the victim. It is rather a dynamic process. At the same time the way in which a child responds to such severe risk situations influences the interactions with his or her environment. Several authors stress the importance of the relationship of parent and child variables to child outcomes (Hammen, Burge & Stansbury, 1990; Hart & Brassard, 1986).

The anxious attachment or the failure of the child to attach to an adult are the results of a process in which the child, with his or her unique equipment, has found a kind of balance in severe risk situations. The child defends itself with primitive coping mechanisms, when such risk situations started at a very early stage in life. Such primitive coping or defense mechanisms are for example masking sensory input, splitting, avoiding or keeping away from people or counterfobic behaviour. On the one hand these mechanisms can be aggravated or attenuated by initial tendencies in the child itself like great anxiety, limited resilience, temperament, hypersensitivity or having a tendency towards a lesser degree of object relatedness. On the other hand resilience to or the ability to break down parental neglect can also depend on genetically determined characteristics like adaptability or having a tendency to a greater degree of object relatedness. Individual differences may protect an individual from development of psychiatric disorders in such severe risk situations like neglect and abuse (Rutter, 1977).

Psychopathology as a result of maltreatment can be conceived as a 'relational psychopathology' (Cicchetti & Rizley, 1981; Sameroff & Chandler, 1975) and a developmental psychopathology.

Treatment is aimed at responding to basic needs, taking away the hindrance to and providing preconditions for further development. The primitive coping mechanisms must be handled in such a way as to give the child as yet a chance to develop the different social modalities. The various developmental theories give clues for treatment-plans and therefore treatment is necessarily eclectic. From this point of view possibilities and impossibilities for development can be described for each child. In the Child and Adolescent Psychiatric Clinic of the Sophia Children's Hospital more than 120 children were admitted in the last twenty years for residential treatment. Of the 63 children who were admitted during the last ten years 40% has been seriously maltreated, most of them emotionally neglected and physically abused. We have tried to develop a systematic description of our experiences during the treatment of these children.

The phase-model we propose gives way to assess the duration of admittance and the preconditions for future social environment to guarantee the child's further personality development.

5.2 Spectrum of psychopathology

The developmental lines can be very differently influenced by maltreatment. A process starts from early traumatic events. The first contact and relationship with human beings can be very seriously damaged. If a child fails to master important developmental tasks, subsequent adaptation during the next developmental level will also be impaired. The same parental act will have a different impact on the child at different developmental levels (Garbarino et al, 1986).

As mentioned above, the effects of such severe risk events on the personality development of the child can be very different, because development starts from the biological core of the child itself. The interaction between the infant's congenital equipment and early experiences will lead to the emergence of fundamental trends in the child. These fundamental trends give rise to and intertwine with later emotional and social development (Weil, 1970). Constitutional variations explain why not every child responds in the same way to the same kind of neglect or abuse.

In residential treatment the behaviour pattern of long-lasting duration of a maltreated child is not regarded as a static and fixed condition. There is a broad range of behaviours which cannot all be contained within any single diagnostic category.

Aichhorn (1936) emphasized in his book 'Wayward Youth' that there is a hindrance in two important steps in emotional and social development:

- internal and external factors which prevent the normal growth of the various ego functions act as a hindrance to the 'primary adaptation to reality', which Aichhorn regards as the basis of emotional development;
- internal and external factors which interfere with the emotional development prevent the child to attach his feelings to permanent love-objects. Where normal emotional ties are missing, there is little incentive nor is it possible for the child to model itself on the pattern of the adult world which surrounds it. It fails to build up the identification which should become the core of a strong and sufficient superego, that can act as a barrier against the instinctual forces and guide its behaviour in accordance with social standards.

Emotional maladjustment may thus become manifest as severe as a psychosis (disintegration). Symptomatic behaviour as result of central nervous system damage has also to be considered.

It is useful define the behaviour pattern on a spectrum of disturbances. Constitutional factors, the family's response to temperamental characteristics and earlier unresolved reactive disturbances interact to produce the symptom picture. Important factors are to be considered such as the child's age, his level of emotional and social development and any previous experiences which may sensitize him to specific events. In this way it may be recognized that emotional and social coping mechanisms, arising in the early life of the maltreated child, may blend with mechanisms arising from constitutional vulnerability.

Within the broad spectrum of symptomatology of child neglect and abuse it is possible according to our experience to discern four levels of psychopathology:

1. disadvantageous characteristics of the child which remain 'weak' as a result of early deficits in the parent-child relationship,
2. specific organic and/or constitutional disorders,
3. persisting of original defense mechanisms and
4. intertwining of the various developmental aspects.

A child may show a complex mixture of these four main areas:

Ad 1. Certain aspects in the 'basic core' of the child like greater anxiety potential, hypersensitivity, little adaptability, which can be recognized as characteristics in later life (Weil, 1970), partially determine individual nuances of the symptomatology. The early interaction between the infant's equipment and the parental neglect and/or abuse will result in various degrees of further imbalance and vulnerability. Considering this basic core in the evaluation of our patients may help to unravel the intertwined development and to clarify some of the often rather diffuse diagnostic aspects;

Ad 2. A disturbance in one aspect of development can influence other domains of development. For instance, insufficient 'pre-speech' or lack of stimulation of language in the first years of life can cause problems not only in the language development of the child but can also give rise to apathy or lack of pleasure in functioning in relation to others (Provence & Lipton, 1962). Brazelton (1974) described the importance of 'pre-speech' in the early mother infant reciprocity. A lesser speech development can cause serious problems in school performance;

Ad 3. Primitive defense mechanisms or coping mechanisms can be recognized as a defense against the frightening reality. Original defense (e.g. counterfobic behaviour) can be seen to form the later core of the psychopathology (Rieker & Carmen, 1986). The profound disconfirmation of reality, exclusion of the memory or knowledge what was done to the child, form obstacles for an integrated identity which can be understood as the impact of the frightening reality on the young child's developing personality structure;

Ad 4. Organic and constitutional disorders such as dyslexia or attention deficit disorder are often masked by the symptomatology of emotional and social maladjustment. Hyperactivity can be seen in this context as a primitive way to channel stress, but an underlying constitutional attention deficit disorder can also be considered. On the one hand blocking of memory and thoughts can cause reading problems, on the other hand psychological testing and family history can give clues for dyslexia.

In our opinion residential treatment is aimed at recognition of underlying sources of maladaptation and suggests ways of appropriate intervention. The behaviour is not the target of treatment, but the underlying intrapsychic mechanisms. The children who were admitted in our child psychiatric ward because of psychopathology as a result of maltreatment, were victimized early in their lives. A specific dynamic process started in early life as result of the maltreatment. As a result of an early disturbed parent-child relationship the child will be at risk of an early instability with regard to such fundamental rhythms as feeding, elimination, sleeping and waking. Congenital factors can contribute to this instability. This regulatory instability can still be found in later life.

An early disturbed interaction between the parent and the child aggravates or attenuates initial tendencies, such as the quick switching of mood, anxiety potential, perceptual sensitivity and responsiveness, insufficient integrative function or potential for neutralization. A primitive way of canalization of stress can remain as screaming, running and hyperactivity. The pleasure-displeasure balance shifts in favour of displeasure, as the child experienced early and persistent distress. The unpleasant physical feelings become part of the self. The child experiences no pain or extraordinarily pain in different situations. Automutilation and head banging can take place. The forerunner of later integrative function can be damaged, because the infant needs his parents for developing this potential. Therefore, fundamental and basic needs are also to be supplied during treatment. Considering the foregoing these needs are intertwined with those forthcoming out of the basic core of the child.

The picture of clinical reality can be best described as: 'everything is possible' and 'some children can make the most out of the least, while others need the most to arrive at very little'.

5.3   Symptomatology in a developmental model

Treatment of the maltreated child is in our opinion based on specific knowledge of the developmental possibilities and impossibilities of the individual child. This will do justice to the kaleidoscopic variety of influences which lead different children into maladaptive behaviour and the tremendous diversity of dynamic patterns in behaviourial disorders. Almost all children and adolescents present problematic behaviour which at initial presentation do not seem promising at all.

Using a developmental model can be helpful to clarify which aspects of the pathological development are treatable and which conditions are necessary to provide a base for further development. It even allows predictions about future vulnerabilities and conditions for maintenance of development.

Development can be differentiated in three or four important domains or main-axes (Figure 1). Starting at birth with a certain specific physiologic 'luggage', the biologic core (Weil, 1970), a child's development differentiates in the first years of life in a biological-somatic (at first with a strong accent on motor development), a cognitive and an emotional axis. In our opinion only later in life, when reciprocity and later mutuality comes into existence, a social developmental axis will gradually emerge. The social developmental axis is considered by different investigators as the same as the emotional. All other developmental traces, for instance development of play, language or morality can be placed among these four axes.

Almost all problems of the neglected and/or abused child can be ordered on the four main axes of the developmental differentiation shown in Figure 1. A fusion between the biological-somatic, cognitive and emotional-social aspects of development characterize the behaviour of maltreated children.

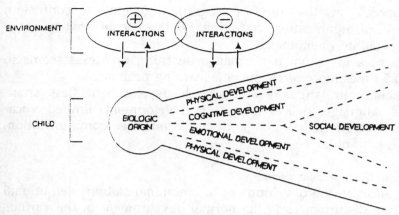

Figure 1   The developmental differentiation

The different aspects of symptomatology can be ordered in the four, above mentioned, developmental domains.

5.3.1 The biological-somatic development
- Disturbances of bodily growth (failure-to-thrive syndrome, aggravation of diseases by neglect of medical care).
- Physical complaints (primary stress response, physical abuse).
- Disturbances in the development and maturation of the central nervous system (mental retardation, neurological abnormalities).
- Disturbances in the regulation of attention and activity level (long-lasting attention deficits, arousal phenomena).
- Disturbances in the development of the sensory system (raising of sensory thresholds, high perceptual sensitivity and responsiveness, a lack of recognizable expressions between mother and abused infant, dissociation and altered states of consciousness).
- Disturbances in the sensory-motor development (restraint of experimenting, less interaction on a physical level).

5.3.2 The cognitive development
- Disturbances in cognitive developmental potentials (deficits in IQ-performance, disturbances in memory).
- Disturbances in cognitive-structural development (deficits in conservation performance, cognitive maladaptation to a changing environment).

- Disturbances in the use of cognition (cognitive confusion, psychotic disorganization, cognition for the use of anxiety regulation, avoidant phenomena).
- Disturbances in school performance (learning problems seems to occur 3.5 times more often, specific learning problems).
- Disturbances in language and speech development (less spontaneous language, delays in speech development, limited vocabulary, poor internal language, distorted affective communication, verbal inhibition).

5.3.3 The emotional development
- Disturbances in the development of emotional stability (emotional instability, disturbances in the normal development of the various ego functions, ego disorganization, disturbances of the self concept).
- Disturbances in attachment and self-constancy (ambivalent attachments, basic mistrust, internalizing of the abusive object relationships, poorer self-esteem and self-image, splitting in 'good' and 'bad').
- Disturbances of affect (reexperiencing phenomena, depressive symptoms, dissociative phenomena, secondary narcissism).
- Extensive use of primitive defense mechanisms (identification with the aggressor, avoidance, raising of sensory thresholds, denial, projection, splitting and isolation, counterfobic behaviour, punishment seeking behaviour, heightened externality).
- Disturbances in the regulation of aggressive drives (repression of anger, impaired impulse control, masochistic and self-destructive behaviour);
- Disturbances in the superego development (the child's conclusion can be that the maltreatment is caused by his/her own badness). Anger, feelings of guilt, disturbed moral development can be the result of a disturbed relation to the self, the primary caretakers and the rest of the world (no love relations).

5.3.4 The social development
- Disturbances in social behaviour (more negative and lesser positive interactions, reduced social skills, aggressive behaviours as well as social withdrawal).
- Difficulties in relating to parents and peers (more opposition to

parental interventions, ambivalent loyalties).

5.4 Application in residential treatment

Eissler (1959) noted that neglected and abused children seldom show any motivation to go into treatment. Defense mechanisms and strategies like denying to assign meaning to the abuse, to know or remember what was done to them or to claim powerful affects that might be expected of the abuse become obstacles for treatment (Rieker & Carmen, 1986). They even seem to enjoy the way they behave. For these children there is no reason to give up their primitive defense mechanisms. These mechanisms have become part of their personality and there is no awareness about the reasons of their dysfunctioning.

A logical succession of sub-phases can be derived from our experience the last twenty years with the treatment of neglected and/or abused children, who are not able to profit sufficiently from the interaction and relationship with others, just because of their defense mechanisms.

The child is in desperate need to hold on to the promise of the good and loving parent (Shengold, 1979). This causes great difficulties in facing the reality and gives rise to enormous conflicts in the child with strong feelings of loyalty towards the parent.

The treatment of these children in the Child and Adolescent Psychiatric Clinic of our hospital can characterized by a logical construction of sub-phases, which we have tried to describe systematically.

Phase 1: Structure and love

Physical care, a structured daily programm with structured activities and regularity of daily activities in the proximity of adults with a loving attitude provide a base for new experiences for the child with its own body and functioning. This equals what Erikson (1963) called 'I am what I'm given'. Too close emotional contact gives rise to old defense mechanisms, because the child expects every adult to be as its parents. The child needs its own territory.

Phase 2: Offering a new reality

By explaining to the child that the parents are the biological parents but no longer the educators we can provide a possibility for the child to express its feelings of anger and impotence without being afraid of the consequences of the utterance of those feelings in relation to its parents, like revenge etcetera. We call this the concept of 'split loyalty'.

Because of its 'old' coping strategies like justification of the parent's cruel acts on the basis of its own bad behaviour the child only gradually can accept this new reality, at first testing the limits of the situation.

In these two first phases and part of the next phase avoidant phenomena must be taken into account. Avoidant phenomena can be recognized as psychogenic amnesia, efforts to avoid associated situations or loss of developmental skills by diminished interest in significant activities (Scannel, 1991). It is important to tell the child that he or she is the only one who knows what happened to him or her. In case of physical contact it is necessary to explain always the reason for it and to assure that no harm will take place.

Paradoxically, in a safety-providing and structured climate, the child will show arousal phenomena, like hypervigilance, irritability, poor concentration or sleeping disturbances. These arousal phenomena will only gradually disappear.

Phase 3: Old and new coping strategies

Gradually, sometimes this can take months, the structured context will become meaningful to the child. The child sometimes abandons its original coping strategies. Some children have serious problems with sphincter control. Social modalities like 'keeping and let go' (Erikson, 1963) can be gradually recognized. Moments of pleasure and comfortable experiences are still very quickly disrupted by a negative and aggressive mood. It is important to confirm in a positive way the former situation of pleasure and comfort. Negative interactions must be prevented or stopped as soon as possible. Situations become clear for which the child is sensitized due to experiences in the past. It is very important to prevent or stop those situations as well.

In the last part of this phase it is important to prevent or interrupt the so-called re-experiencing phenomena (Scannel, 1991), like repetitive play with aggression and destruction.

Phase 4: Autonomy

Reflection on his part in (looking for) negative interactions is little by little stimulated. The effect of his own behaviour in positive interactions is positively confirmed. Gradually the child's autonomy is furthered by showing him his old way of interacting and the results of his developing possibilities of positive interactions. New strategies will emerge. A positive interaction can also be the acceptance of help of an adult instead of over-independency. The child can learn that with the help of the adult difficult situations can be mastered or solved, but it takes long before the child can really profit from this skill. It is a phase in which the child needs much emotional corrective experiences.

Phase 5: Starting new relations

Gradually the child will be able to leave negative interactions or even choose for positive solutions because of his developing relationship with important persons. Still the over-independency is very strong. A depressive mood is now observable: the child no longer has to defend itself against the emotional pain caused by its history of abandonment, neglect or abuse. The child starts asking questions about 'why me?'. The child now can express and work through its feelings of inferiority. In this very phase the child typically seeks closer contact and dependency by showing minor physical complaints. Conflicts with the environment gradually shift into conflicts within the child. The child suffers for the first time directly from the emotional 'pain' because of his problems. First attempts of reflection on its own actions and reactions in relation with others starts.

The periods of depression outstand the periods of aggression and negative interactions. Periods of positive feelings and positive identification will gradually predominate.

Phase 6: Attachment behaviour

Traces of attachment behaviour can now be recognized. For the first time the child cries when it hurts itself, follows with its eyes the coming and leaving of important persons, asks questions about these persons, where they live or what they do when they are not at work. It makes more meaningful eye-contact and chooses for the proximity of the adult when it is in stress.

It can be recognized that the child has difficulties in keeping his needs for proximity and contact within one person for a longer period. Sometimes it still can be necessary for the child to split: to keep positive contact with one person and to behave very negatively with the other.

From this point there is a differentiation into two tracks or sub-phases until phase 9. The first track (A) is more based on working-through and insight on the part of the child. The other track (B) is more directed towards influencing behaviour through behaviourial therapy principles and covering the past instead of working-through and insight. A child can shift from track A to B and vice versa, depending on his cognitive abilities, flexibility, temperament, resilience to regression, concomitant organic brain dysfunctions like attention deficit disorder or environmental factors.

On track A a child will start to develop a more positive self-image and more self-esteem. It can refer to its own body as a good frame of reference to reach out to the surrounding world. These positive feelings will alternate with the fear for regression to old mechanisms, where incidentally anxiety or paranoid feelings predominate again. Sometimes the child is really testing his own limits to prove to itself that 'it is not the same child any more'.

Phase 7A: Reconstruction of the personality

Attachment, even ambiguous, grows. It is important to explain to the child that every human being has his 'good' and 'bad' sides. Gradually the child can learn to accept his 'good' side next to his 'bad' side. Integration of these aspects and reorientation on the past reconstruct its personality. There is an increasing insight of his 'bad' side as a result of adverse experiences in the past. The child learns to express his feelings of anger in more acceptable ways. Feelings of sadness, loneliness and solitude can be expressed in symbolic play. The past comes into 'existence' in daily expressions of the child and he starts to ask questions. Right now the child starts for the first time in his life to think about the future ('Where am I going to live?' 'Will there be persons who are able to love me?')

Phase 7B:

The child learns and experiences the positive effect on his or her surroundings to withdraw from aggressive acts. Instead, more acceptable expressions of aggression are stimulated. Moments of anger can be reflected on from the side of the adult together with the child, at first after a while, later on the moment itself. It is helpful to start a rewarding system. The child can be stimulated to think about his or her future in structured conversations.

Phase 8A: Self-confidence and self-esteem

More permanent and long-lasting changes in behaviour of the child can now be recognized. Positive identification with important adults is necessary to help the child accept reality and to cope with the demands from its environment. Reflection on and verbalization of difficult situations is now possible. Past, here-and-now and future fit together. The old coping strategies now belong to the past. Another step in growing self-confidence and self-esteem is taken. Pleasure in autonomous functioning and mastery are very important aspects of daily activities. This stage equals what Erikson (1963) called 'I am who I want to be'. There is a need to amuse itself and to learn to play with other children. The child asks for a club or hobby.

Phase 8B:

Possibilities for autonomous functioning are gradually offered in an increasing social environment. A "coincidental meeting" can be arranged to stimulate the child to get into a hobby or to join a club.

Phase 9A: Secondary acquired security

Independently functioning now based on secondary acquired security starts. In stead of the primary basic mistrust new feelings of safety are created. The child even feels safe enough to take opposite positions with respect to the meaningful adults. It even enjoys to play with opposition and there is a real joy of victory. There is pleasure and motivation to learn at school. The child wants compliments for his achievements. Because the child needs the reliability of knowing where it will be growing up (Maluccio, Fein & Olmstead, 1986) permanency planning with placement in a foster-home is necessary. We are used to find a 'weekend-family' for the child as an intermediary step in this permanency planning.

The aim of the last part of treatment (track A) must be to help the child to recall the neglect and/or abuse and its original affects in a safe and controlled way and to restore the accurate meanings attached to it. The turning point occurs when his or her rage is not experienced as meaningless but as a response to cruelty. The work of therapy is now to reclaim that traumatic past as a part of one's history and identity. Then the child will be able to grieve and to leave both the trauma and the distortions in memory and affects that once were necessary for survival. Sometimes this phase only takes place after many years after discharge.

Phase 9B:

During the last phase of treatment the child can show old behaviour patterns again. It is important to anticipate with the child on this possibility in several conversations, to reassure the child that it is temporary and to emphasize all the new ways of behaviour the child has learned. For the child the past must be clearly distinguished from the future, in such a way that the child can be convinced that he or she can handle future situations and that the past will not repeat itself. The child must have a clear view on what it can learn from the adults and how it can reach these goals.

5.5 Summary

There is a broad spectrum of symptomatology of maltreated children. The core problem is a relational and developmental psychopathology starting in the first years of life.
The underlying mechanisms of the problems and the behaviour of these children are characterized by a fusion of biological-somatic, cognitive and emotional-social aspects of development.
Treatment is aimed at offering basic needs, taking away the hindrance on development and to provide preconditions for further development. The primitive coping mechanisms must be handled in such a way as to give the child as yet a chance to develop the different social modalities. The various developmental theories give clues for treatment-plans and therefore treatment is necessarily eclectic. A concrete course of action and treatment-plans and short-term as well as long-term (permanency) planning are needed.
This article offers a phase-model based on an explicative description of experiential knowledge. In this phase-model possibilities and impossibilities for development can be described for each child as well as an estimation of duration of treatment. To understand the logical succession of phases during treatment will help to overcome discouragement from the part of the staff members as result of depression, somatic complaints or reexperiencing phenomena of the child.
New mechanisms must emerge, not only in the child but also in the health care workers to cope with feelings of despair. Instead we can have more self-esteem en self-confidence in our own treatment-plans when they will be based on a systematic description of the course of treatment.

References

Aichhorn, A. (1936). *Wayward youth*. New York: Viking Press.

Brazelton, T. (1974). The origins of reciprocity: the early mother-infant interaction. In M. Lewis, & L. Rosenblum [eds.], *The effect of the infant on its caregiver, Volume 1* (pp. 49-76). New York: John Wiley.

Cicchetti D., & Rizley, A. (1981). Developmental perspectives on the etiology, intergenerational transmission, and sequelae of child maltreatment. *New Directions for Child Development, 11*, 31-55.

Dennis, W. (1938). Infant development under conditions of restricted practice and of minimum social stimulation: a preliminary report. *Journal of Genetic Psychology, 53*, 149-158.

Eissler, K.R. (1959). Some problems of delinquency. In K.R. Eissler [ed.], *Searchlights on delinquency* (p. 9). New York: International Universities Press.

Erikson, E.H. (1963). *Childhood and society*. New York: Norton.

Garbarino, J., Guttman, E., & Seeley, J. (1986). *The psychologically battered child*. San Francisco: Jossey-Bass.

Hammen, C., Burge, D., & Stansbury, K. (1990). Relationship of mother and child variables to child outcomes in a high-risk sample: a causal modelling analysis. *Developmental Psychology, 26*, 24-30.

Hart, S.N., & Brassard, M.R. (1986). *Developing and validating operationally defined measures of emotional maltreatment: a multimodel study of the relationship between caretaker behaviors and children characteristics across three developmental levels* (Grant No. DHHS 90CA1216). Washington, DC: DHHS and NCCAN.

Johnson, C.F. (1990). Child abuse and the child psychiatrist. In B.D. Garfinkel, G.A. Carlson, & E.B. Weller [eds.], *Psychiatric disorders in children and adolescents* (pp. 339-358). Philadelphia: W.B. Saunders Company.

Maluccio, A.N., Fein, E., & Olmstead, K.A. (1986). *Permanency planning for children*. New York: Tavistock Publications.

Provence, S., & Lipton, R. (1962). *Infants in institutions*. New York: International Universities Press.

Rieker, A.P., & Carmen, E.H. (1986). The victim-to-patient process: the disconfirmation and transformation of abuse. *American Journal of Orthopsychiatry, 56*, 360-370.

74

Rutter, M. (1977). Individual differences. In M. Rutter & L. Hersov [eds.], *Child psychiatry: modern approaches*. London, Blackwell Scientific Publications.

Sameroff, A., & Chandler, M. (1975). Reproductive risk and the continuum of caretaking casualty. In F. Horowitz [ed.], *Review of child development research, volume 4* (pp. 197-244). Chicago: University of Chicago Press.

Scannell, T.D. (1991, September). *Some thoughts upon the abused to abuser continuum*. Poster presented on the ESCAP-conference, London.

Shengold, L.L. (1979). Child abuse and deprivation: soul murder. *Journal of the American Psychoanalytic Association, 27*, 533-559.

Weil, A.P. (1970). The basic core. *The Psychoanalytic Study of the Child, 25*, 442-460.

6   Residential Care for Sexually Abused Adolescents

F.A.E. Pannekoek

6.1   Introduction

This chapter examines the need for finding a method of guidance and treatment for sexually abused adolescents who are in residential care.

It briefly describes the results of research into the phenomenon of sexually abused young people in three centres for residential treatment in the Netherlands[1]. These results emphasize the need to pay specific attention to the development of a method for dealing with this group of abused adolescents within the residential care system.

For the development of the proposed basic approach, previously available knowledge of signals and consequences of sexual abuse has been used (Lesnik-Oberstein, 1986; Driessen, 1986; Platvoet & Dubbink, 1988). In addition to this, group leaders and staff members of the three residential centres mentioned above made an important contribution by discussing their treatment[2].

After discussing the treatment, we will examine the question of whether the treatment makes certain demands on the group leaders who have to realize the methodology within the group. Finally we look at the need for an improvement in know-how.

---

[1] The centres involved in the investigation are 'De Amerberg' (Amersfoort), 'Nieuw-Maliesteijn'(Utrecht) and 'Zandbergen' (Amersfoort).

[2] Special thanks go to R. Schoemaker and B. Hiestand, group leaders who made a special contribution by discussing their approach with the adolescents of their group, several of whom had been sexually abused.

In discussing our approach we follow the treatment phases characteristic for our centres.

When speaking about guidance of young people we are referring in
particular to boys and girls aged 10 to 18.

We speak of adolescents and group leaders in the feminine form, but
one can also think of boys and male group leaders.

The working method presented is mainly a reaction to the current
state of affairs within our centres and serves as a basis for the
individual planning of treatment, which is different for every young
person.

6.2 Research into the phenomenon of sexually abused adolescents in residential care

In 1991 we researched the phenomenon of sexually abused young
people in our residential centres. 167 children and adolescents were
involved in the research. At the time of the investigation they had
been in one of the centres for at least three months. Of the 96 boys
involved in the investigation 6 (6%) had definitely been abused and
5 more (5%) were suspected of having been abused. Of the 71 girls
15 (21%) had definitely been abused and there were suspicions of
abuse regarding 12 more (17%).[1]

This means that for close to a quarter of our youth we should take
into account the possible effects of sexual abuse. These percentages
justify the additional attention to the care and guidance of sexually
abused young people in residential care.

6.3 Sexual abuse as a subject for the intake

At an intake it is usually considered important to invite those who
are directly involved in the placement process. These are always the
young person, often with her parents, and the mediator who assists

---

[1] Insofar as the identity of perpetrators was known, 68% of them were parents,
step-parents or partners of a parent, 18% were relatives of the family, and 15%
were younger persons.

in the placement. The presence of the people involved increases the chance of agreeing on the definition of the problem, the formulation of goals and the choice of methods of treatment. Agreement increases the chance of cooperation from the people involved. Consequently the chances of success are predictably increased.

In an intake procedure dealing with sexually abused adolescents, the interview has to take place without the parents more frequently than with adolescents who have not been abused. It could be too intimidating or frightening for the young person to be confronted with the perpetrator or the parent who allowed the abuse to continue with or without awareness. However this does not mean that one can eliminate the parents from the intake phase. A separate consultation with the parents can be arranged without the young person's presence. When even the presence of the parents in the centre is regarded as too threatening for the young person, this can take place outside the institution.

When abuse is evident before the intake or is the reason for placement, it is appropriate to talk about the abuse at the intake interview. This is assuming we regard the intake phase as the moment when the problem is defined and objectives and working methods are agreed upon. The presence of a possible perpetrator at the admission interview is no reason not to ask about abuse. In fact, there is even more reason to ask about it then, so that the young person can see that within the institution people will not reinforce the fear that generally exists among victims with regard to the perpetrators.

The investigation and our experience show that adolescents seldom talk about abuse during the intake interview, even when they are invited to do so. The adolescents say that they do not see the intake interview as the appropriate moment to talk about abuse for the first time; after all, a relationship of trust has not yet been established with the adults.

Nevertheless there are reasons mentioned by Thie (1987) for asking questions about abuse during an admission interview, even when nothing is yet known. 'It becomes clear to the young person that within the institution people are aware of the issue and are open to it. Because this is a standard question in the intake procedure, the young person knows that she is not the only one who has to cope with this problem' (p. 29).

Within the framework of specifying problems and objectives, questions about abuse can be part of a series of standard questions during admission. The subject of sexual abuse should especially be explored if a psychological examination takes place during the intake.

Adolescents who have been dealing with abuse within the family are often troubled by feelings of guilt and feel themselves partly responsible for the consequences their institutionalization has on the family. We know that the emotional confusion this can cause can lead to decompensation and even to suicidal tendencies. Therefore adolescents should be told in the intake phase that no actions regarding the family will be taken without the their involvement or knowledge.

Should the person who does the intake be a man or a woman? There is a chance that a man may raise fears in a young person. Our experience shows that one should not jump to that conclusion. When the information regarding the intake leads one to think that the young person will be more at ease with a female or a male, then that can be taken into account. When no preference is known one can ask about it. In doubtful cases two people can conduct the intake.

6.4   Coping with suspicions of sexual abuse after admission

It has already been mentioned that in many cases the suspicion of sexual abuse arises only after the adolescent has been admitted.

At the first sign that this may have occurred, the group leaders must take a number of actions simultaneously. They should consult with one another and with a staff member. During the consultation observations can be exchanged and arrangements can be made for further observations.

The staff member must establish whether these signs might possibly be the result of another problem. This prevents jumping to the conclusion that sexual abuse is the problem and overlooking other problems and objectives for admission that may exist.

Following the consultations with the team abuse can be brought up as a special issue in the family investigation if earlier or supplementary diagnosis of the young person warrants this.

6.5 Talking about sexual abuse

Internal research shows that three months after the intake 24% of the young people known to have been sexually abused were still unwilling to discuss it. Before abuse can be discussed, a number of conditions must be satisfied; the young person must feel safe before she can talk about the abuse.

One should give the young person time to test the group leaders and to build up a confidential relationship. It must become clear to the girl that she can discuss any subject with the group leaders. This becomes more obvious when talking about more intimate subjects within the group. Sometimes a girl will suddenly dare to speak about her own experiences of sexual abuse following a general discussion in the group about sexuality or sexual abuse.

The social worker may also find it difficult to talk about such matters. Consultation with colleagues is then important to enable one to discuss such insecurity. Before one can speak about abuse with young people, it is necessary to learn to speak about sexuality. It is often necessary to have concrete examples of questions that could be asked.

6.6 Resistance in the first interview

The difficulty young people have in talking about abuse varies. This should be taken into account. Experience shows that one can ask adolescents whether they want to tell their own story or whether they would prefer to be asked questions. When a young person dreads the idea of telling her story to everyone, it is useful to appoint a person whom she wants to take into her confidence.

For a number of reasons a request for secrecy cannot be granted indefinitely. In the first place one would set the wrong example by appearing to support perpetrator's wish to remain anonymous. In the second place, secrecy can also cause problems for the social worker if she herself needs assistance in order to help the young person. It is better to discover the motives behind the request for secrecy so that something can be done about it.

Acceptance is an element that characterizes every good interview but is absolutely indispensable in an interview with sexually abused adolescents. The emotions of the social worker can get in the way of acceptance. A young person's story about sexual abuse often arouses strong emotions from the group leaders. 'The logical reactions are indignation, rage and identification with the victim, but these reactions will not help find a solution', says Lamers-Winkelman (1986, p. 633). A group leader writes: 'Looking back, I was carried away too much by my own emotions, standards and values. They clashed with her feelings of loyalty towards her father' (Thie, 1988, p. 33). It can be helpful for social workers to distinguish between the bond the young person still experiences with the parents and the abuse that took place. When the young person's feelings of loyalty are not accepted, one risks having the young person experience the rejection of her roots as a rejection of herself and this could strengthen a negative self-image. Besides that, feelings of guilt might increase because of disapproval, especially when the young person feels co-responsible for things that have happened or when positive experiences are part of the inner confusion. Finally, feelings of guilt could result in the young person preferring to withhold the rest of the story.

In interviews with adolescents it may be necessary to set limits, particularly in the first interview. This is advisable when it appears that disclosure is causing too much tension in the young person. By arranging a second interview, one also prevents the young person from thinking that everything has been discussed and that nothing more will have to be said about the subject. It may also be necessary to set limits when the young person makes demands on the person whom she has taken into her confidence and uses the interviews chiefly as a means of getting attention. A final reason for setting limits is to prevent other aspects of the treatment from being pushed to the background.

6.7 Aspects of guidance within the group

In the following section issues directly related to the guidance of the adolescents within the group will be discussed.

6.7.1 Remaining silent about the abuse
Research has shown that 23% of the young people refuse to talk

about abuse although they admit to having been abused. This is a problem, especially when the young person is suffering because of the abuse. However when we force a young person to talk we may also be guilty of a kind of violation.

Nonetheless, continued silence is a signal that we must look for the cause of the silence. It may be connected to feelings of guilt and shame or an obligation to secrecy. There is a chance that the young person will dare to speak once the background of the silence has been discussed. Sometimes the offer of individual or group therapy provides a solution.

6.7.2 Treating those who wish to return home prematurely

Often when adolescents have only recently been admitted and have come directly from the family into the residential centre, we see the tendency to return home again after a short time.

This alerts us to show understanding for the difficulty that the young person is experiencing in having to remain at the centre. We must discover why the young person wishes to return home. Feelings of loyalty have to be discussed.

It may also be necessary to call in the assistance of the mediator who assisted in the placement process or to take the matter to court if it involves placement of a person who wants to leave.

6.7.3 Sexualizing of relationships

Our research shows that the sexualizing of relationships is the most recurring problematic behaviourial pattern resulting from sexual abuse: it is seen as a symptom in 39% of the children who have either been abused or are suspected of having been abused. Lesnik-Oberstein (1986) writes: 'It is the only way they know to attract attention and it is undoubtedly the result of having been taught that sexual conduct is expected of them' (p. 29). It can be regarded as a shortcoming in social skills and a lack of insight into the consequences of their own behaviour.

It is a signal to the group leaders to confront the young person with the consequences of her behaviour without blaming her.

Group discussions can play an important role as well. The difference between attention, love and sexuality is one subject that could be discussed. In discussions with each other, adolescents can learn to widen their repertoire of behaviour. It has also proved useful to

82

discuss within the group the consequences of sexual abuse in general and to make the adolescents sensitive to the risks of sexualizing behaviour. When such discussions can be held in the open, adolescents appear to be able to understand each other's behaviour better. As a consequence they will probably be more careful in interpreting each other's sexualizing behaviour.

An additional difficulty emerges when the young person demonstrates sexualizing or affectionate behaviour aimed at attracting the attention of a group leader. One must be particularly careful in giving physical attention to abused adolescents. The young person can learn from the group leader that it is also possible to ask for and to receive attention in other ways. Of course, colleagues must also be able to bring this to the attention of the group leader. However this calls for open-mindedness within the team, which cannot occur if a taboo still exists about such issues. It could be a subject for supervision.

6.7.4 Over-emphasis on the abuse

Often it appears that the sexual abuse is part of other problems. The youngster should not dwell on abuse to the exclusion of other problems.

Even when the abuse is the most important problem, it does not automatically mean that the subject should get all the attention. Some of the adolescents still have egos that are too weak to cope with a discussion of the abuse. Inner confusion might increase. In such cases it is preferable to provide an opportunity for positive development. It might be better to focus on a more concrete goal such as obtaining a certificate, thereby increasing self-confidence. After that attention should again be given to coping with the abuse.

6.7.5 Relationship between therapy and guidance within the group

Within our institutions adolescents can have therapy or individual counselling outside the group.

The counselling often forms a necessary adjunct to guidance within the group, and not only because of the assumed professionalism of the therapist. Individual counselling outside the group can be less threatening for a young person because she knows that the issue will not be discussed with those she meets in daily life. In a way the young person herself still has control over her story. In that sense the therapy can also be regarded as a phase in the treatment. It is possible that as a result of the therapy the young person will learn to talk about the subject outside the therapy room.

The discussion outside the group can offer the young person more space because, in contrast to the pedagogical relationship with group leaders, there are no demands in the relationship with the therapist. These additional discussions outside the group may allow her to distinguish between the consequences of the abuse on her present functioning and dealing with the abuse which took place in the past.

It is particularly important to make this distinction when the young person is in danger of assuming the role of a victim, and the abuse begins to control her whole life so that other objectives of treatment are pushed to the background.

6.7.6 Assistance in reporting

Reporting sexual abuse to the authorities is often an enormous step with far-reaching consequences. The main task of a group leader is not to stimulate reporting but to assist in it. Together with the young person the objective of the report should be verified. Once the objective has been determined they can discuss the extent to which the report can be a means of reaching that objective. It must be made clear that reporting seldom fulfils the need to gain recognition for the damage suffered. Verrijn Stuart (1990) says on the subject: 'A lawsuit causes so much pain, so much sorrow, so many imputations - one should never foster the illusion that criminal justice can make your life good again' (cited in: Schaepman, 1990, p. 13). The young person must realize in advance what consequences it can have for her, the family situation, and the relation she has with the members of her family.

When the objective of reporting is to force an admission from the perpetrator, one could consider a procedure which is supported by the judiciary: reporting in phases. After an anonymous report in which the name of the perpetrator is not yet mentioned, the perpetrator is given the opportunity to go into therapy. If he refuses, his name will be added to the report, after which he will again be given the opportunity to go into therapy. If the perpetrator refuses again, the report is handed over to the public prosecutor who can give him a last chance to accept treatment.

84

6.8 Demands on the individual social worker

The issue of abused adolescents is often complex and serious and makes specific demands on the social worker.

The issue of whether the social worker should be a man or a woman has already been mentioned. In the residential centre for sexually abused girls in Groningen they have decided to work with women only, referring to what is called '...the complicated feelings of the girls towards the mainly male perpetrators of incest'. A female social worker could also be a good identification model, especially an assistant who herself has been a victim of sexual abuse (Aukema & Hummel, 1990, p. 122).

Platvoet and Dubbink (1988) suggest that the choice of a male or female social worker should depend on the sex of the perpetrator. They consider this a matter of special importance in the disclosure phase, because in this phase the fear of male adults can be extremely great (p. 90).

Foeken (1986) offers a third viewpoint. Generally she argues in favour of a female therapist. A female therapist awakens the complicated feelings of a woman towards a male perpetrator less quickly. Moreover a female therapist can be a positive identification model. On the other hand, the female social worker could strengthen the memories of the mother, who let her daughter down. Finally Foeken mentions the importance of a male therapist who for once does not react to her in an erotic manner (p. 80).

In connection with this Thie (1987) points to the importance of re-establishing a normal image of men: 'It is good to teach the girl to recover her trust in men. Therefore not only women should provide help in cases of incest' (p. 32). Finally, for women abused by a male perpetrator, it can be important in diminishing feelings of guilt, to hear from a *male* therapist that a *man* was responsible for the abuse. In that case the elimination of guilt cannot be interpreted by the victim as a 'common defence of women amongst themselves'.

From the above considerations one can deduce no general rule about the choice of a man or a woman as social worker or group leader. In the first phase one must particularly consider the fear or aversion that a man or a woman can cause. In the course of care it can be meaningful if the victims can benefit from contact with not only female, but male social workers as well. Then they will be able to discover that the blame they feel towards a man or a woman does not necessarily apply to all men or all women. The presence of both male and female group leaders gives the young person the chance to choose the sex of the social worker for herself. In a later phase one can include a social worker of the other sex, which offers the chance to expand the image of men or women in general.

6.9 Progress in know-how about the guidance of sexually abused children

Social workers within the support system for adolescents ask for more know-how regarding the guidance of sexually abused young people. This is primarily the task of training institutes. But the residential centres themselves will have to be able to meet this need as well.

Within our centre the progress in know-how was organized stepwise. First we looked at sex education. During this phase the way in which assistance can be determined and obstructed by our own emotions became clear. After that, we examined the symptoms and consequences of abuse. Further, based on their own know-how and experience, the social workers were themselves able to develop a plan in phases, which served as a first guideline in the assistance of abused adolescents.

Research into the phenomenon of sexual abuse among adolescents in residential care shows that it is necessary to be aware of the possibility of sexual abuse from the very first moment one comes in contact with the youngsters. A possible treatment approach has been presented in this chapter. The description given contains some elements of a general program of care. Actual treatment, on the other hand, will have to be adapted to the circumstances of each residential setting, i.e. to the situation of each juvenile admitted, and should be based on the assessment and diagnosis of individually articulated problems and needs.

86

References

Aukema, B. & Hummel, J. (1990). Geïntegreerde hulp vanuit het opvanghuis voor incestslachtoffers. In H.E.M. Baartman, A. Burgeness & C. Rümke [eds.], *Incest en hulpverlening* (pp. 122-127). Amersfoort/Leuven: Acco.

Driessen, B. (1986). Incest en het jonge meisje. In C. van Lichtenburcht, W. Bezemer & W. Gianotten [eds.], *Verder na incest* (pp. 37-48). Baarn: Ambo.

Foeken, I. (1986). Feministische hulpverlening. In C. van Lichtenburcht, W. Bezemer & W. Gianotten [eds.], *Verder na incest* (pp. 78-86). Baarn: Ambo.

Lamers-Winkelman, F. (1986). Seksueel misbruik van peuters en kleuters. *Tijdschrift voor Orthopedagogiek, 12*, 625-637.

Lesnik-Oberstein, M. (1986). Incest en het jonge kind. In C. van Lichtenburcht, W. Bezemer & W. Gianotten [eds.], *Verder na incest* (pp. 28-36). Baarn: Ambo.

Platvoet, A., & Dubbink, A. (1988). *Incest: hun zorg, jouw zorg.* Groningen: Wolters-Noordhof.

Schaepman, K. (1991). Is aangifte van verkrachting altijd verstandig? *Vrij Nederland, 40*, 13-14.

Thie, C. (1987). *Kan ik er wat aan doen? Over de begeleiding van meisjes met incestervaring.* Baarn: De Jelburg (unpublished).

7 Experiential Education as a Running Start to Social Competence

T.P. Keulen

7.1 Introduction

Adventurous activities can be an unusual but very effective assist-ance project in child care, especially for young people who cannot benefit from more traditional forms of assistance. In this chapter I will report on a practical special assistance project we have devel-oped over the last seven years in our institution: the *Haagse Hervor-mde Kindertehuizen* (HHK), a multi-functional youth care institution in Den Haag.

I will start with the background of the project and the concept of 'experiential education'. Then I will describe the project. Finally I will present some major results of a long-term follow-up investigation.

7.2 The backgrounds of the project

The special assistance project of the HHK was started as an experi-ment in 1984, and was based on the following facts.

We realized that a great - and in our eyes increasing - number of young people were not profiting from our traditional forms of assistance: they could hardly (if at all) be treated in our institution, situated in the city of Den Haag. These were mainly youngsters with severe behaviourial problems (in DSM III terms: conduct disorders). They caused problems in all environments: at home, at school, on the street, but in child care institutions as well. They broke the rules, played hooky, stole, vandalised, were aggressive and violent - in short these kids were very difficult to handle and, as a result, were often placed in closed institutions - mostly located in the country-side. One could say these were youngsters (mostly boys) with very incompetent social behaviour. They failed in all areas of life; they did not really participate in society and their perspectives were quite unfavourable.

We are talking here about youngsters who are not motivated to seek help, who have neither the trust nor the verbal, intellectual and introspectional skills to take advantage of therapeutic interventions, and who are too aggressive and unruly to be treated in a community-based project. Successive experiences of failure have hardened them and made them difficult to reach. One could say they were too difficult and had caused too many problems to be helped in a regular program.

On the other hand during active group holidays with large groups of youngsters who were admitted, we found that precisely those youngsters who displayed maladjusted behaviour in a community-based project in The Netherlands, behaved themselves in a more socially acceptable way in extremely primitive conditions. This strengthened the idea that these circumstances might be helpful for those young people who can no longer be placed in traditional forms of youth care.

We started an experiment in 1984 with a group of six boys and two group leaders. They made a *Survival Trek* for two and a half months in Sweden and Norway. This experiment proved very successful and inspired us to continue with this alternative youth assistance project. Since then the project has been continuously evaluated, adjusted and expanded. We were successful. We got quite a lot of publicity, but there were also some failures and disappointments. We learned from both, and in the process we created a powerful alternative treatment program for youth assistance: a program in which 'hopeless' boys get the opportunity to change the course of their lives radically; a program that stimulates these kids to make their own choices not by compensating for their faults but by activating the healthy parts of their personality. It is, as it were, a tough project for tough guys.

The total program, including introduction and post counselling, lasts about one year. Before I describe the project, I will introduce some basic ideas regarding 'experiential education'.

7.3 Experiential education, some basic ideas

The essence of experiential education is that the educator creates, enhances and manipulates the circumstances a child is placed in, in order to seduce and to stimulate him or her to function at a higher level.

In 'normal' education the significance of the circumstances in which a child grows up is obvious. One thing about which almost all educational theories agree is that these circumstances affect the developmental process. Every child psychologist or educator emphasizes the importance of good circumstances. The positive influence of actively involved parents in a stimulating environment enables the child to reach higher steps in his development.

In child care we have to deal with children and adolescents who have not grown up under normal and positive circumstances. We deal with children who have generally grown up under very bad conditions, and who have not had safe and stimulating contact with their parents, for example children who were neglected, ill-treated and/or abused (cf. chapters 5 and 6). In residential centres we should offer them ample facilities to make up for what they lack; that is to say a rich and warm environment should be created in which social and practical learning processes could compensate for what these children missed in their families.

I say 'should' because often this is not the case. In my opinion the emotional and educational climate in our professional residential care centres must generally be characterized as extremely poor: there is a change of educators every day; there is an atmosphere of inactivity where group leaders resemble the nursing staff of a hospital; the television set is the central point in most group rooms. A blanket of care is offered to compensate for the understandable passivity of the child, but it makes the client totally dependant. Goffman (1961) described it excellently for us. Too many different people try to poke their nose deep into the child's life.

The child is 'on the defensive' and shows aggression, breaks rules and agreements, tests the limits, doubts the intentions of the educators, or...reverts to passivity. The child experiences being cared for, and of course this is important. On the other hand many children miss the experience of being able to influence their own lives, to make their own decisions and to be responsible.

Although the assertion above applies particularly to traditional settings that are relatively isolated from society, sometimes small-scale community-based projects show (some of) the same characteristics. In many residential facilities the treatment approach emphasizes 'compensating for' to the detriment of 'activating and stimulating.'

From the viewpoint of experiential education, residential child care should offer the kids opportunities to gain existential and powerful experiences. In an experiential education project situations and circumstances are created that differ from what the child is used to. The child is confronted with unknown and unexpected situations in which new learning processes can take place. The influence of the educator in the learning process is partly replaced by the influence of the situation; in other words, the influence of the educator becomes manifest in his arrangement of the circumstances.

Of course, all residential treatment programs 'exploit' the situation, and try to create new and better circumstances in which the child can grow. De Ruyter (1983, p.163) emphasizes that 'situation-handling' is one of the main characteristics of residential treatment. A characteristic feature of projects based on experiential education is the confrontation of participants with rather *extreme* and mostly *unknown* circumstances.

In the next section I will describe the survival trek program of the Haagse Hervormde Kindertehuizen.

7.4 Description of the program

In its current format the program lasts about one year (on average) for each client. Based on our experiences of the last eight years and including others' descriptions of experiential education projects[1], we

---

[1] Cf. *'Een voettocht als begeleidingsmiddel'* (1984); Van den Bergh & Scholte (1984); Schellevis (1985); De Vries, Van den Bergh & Scholte (1986); Kraft & Sakofs (1988); *'Overleven in de asfaltjungle'* (1989); Davidson, Redner, Amdur & Mitchell (1990); Ziechenspeck (1990); Du Prie (1991); Helmantel (1991); Helmantel & Hilhorst

have developed a program with four different phases:
Period 1: Information, intake and introduction
Period 2: Survival Trek
Period 3: Training of social skills
Period 4: Post counselling

The basis of the program is a lengthy and gruelling survival trek in Norway. This trek lasts three months, during which the participants and the trek leaders walk about 1500 kilometres, carrying a backpack weighing about 25 kilos on their backs.

7.4.1 Information, intake and introduction
It is very important to prepare the participants for what is going to happen. For most of the participants the project is a 'last chance': it is their last opportunity to take part in a youth assistance project (because they have 'had it all'), and it is their last chance to take their lives into their own hands.

Most participants have the 'choice' of whether to take part in the project or to be placed in a closed institution or a youth prison. Of course this is not an choice between equal alternatives. So we cannot expect the participants to be really motivated; boys or girls (90% of the participants are boys) with a background of more or less forced participation, and with a long 'career' in children's homes, will hardly be motivated to participate.

This plays a major role in the problem of these kids: they have lost their belief and faith in themselves, in adults and in youth assistance, and they have - as a result - landed at the edges of society. Participation in the project should give them a new perspective for the future and the chance to regain confidence in themselves. It should also help them to become more competent and resilient when functioning in the social world.

When (internal) motivation is so relative, part of the program should be to motivate the client (external motivation). This is essential because successful participation in this difficult project is only possible for youngsters who want to fight for it. We invest a lot of

---

(1991); Keulen (1991); and Weg & Bliek (1991).

time in motivating them.

It starts with the first talk, an *information talk*. The potential participant is given quite a lot of information about what the project consists of and what he can expect during the project. After this talk he is asked to write a letter, i.e. to describe the his individual history and to indicate what he expects participation in the program could mean to him.

Of course we do not expect the kid to give a splendid psychological personal analysis. The main point is to activate him or her to think about the project and to reflect upon what should be learned.

In the next conversation, the *intake talk*, we talk about the letter and, more specifically, about what the youngster should learn during the project. At the end of the talk, together with the participant, the individual treatment goals are specified. The participant should think about this: what has to be changed in my life for me to have a better future?

After this talk eight or nine possible participants are brought together on a farm in the countryside for the next phase: the *introduction*. Only six youngsters can leave for Norway, so they all know that not everyone will join the travel group. During the introduction further diagnostics and selection take place.

This period is also used by the staff to stimulate the youngsters' motivation, among others things by preparations for the trek: they learn how to handle the materials they will use in Norway, they are taught how to cook food on a small burner, and they walk a trial trek for a few days. Motivation is also stimulated by a former participant who tells about his experiences within the project, by looking at slides of Norway, etc.

The selection of the boys who will definitely take part in the project depends on how they participate in the introductory program and on the group formation. Potential participants who don't show sufficient intention to take part in the program go back to where they came from: mostly closed residential settings or youth prisons. Possible participants who rehearsed well during the introduction but who dropped out because of the specific formation of the group, are the first participants around when the group for the next project is formed.

Once the group has been formed, the six boys and two trek leaders leave for Norway, to make a Trek that lasts one hundred days.

During this period they walk about 1500 kilometres.

7.4.2 Survival Trek

The start of the Trek is usually quite a shock: the participants - who have grown up with hamburgers, hash and coca-cola - are not used to physical exertion at all. Life during the Trek is virtually the total opposite of the life they live in The Netherlands.

During the Trek they get up very early and they live in the country, isolated from the urban world. They eat dried food that they pick up every eight days. There are no opportunities to escape into the criminality, vandalism or the other forms of deviant behaviour they are used to. They walk about 25 kilometres a day.

The leaders of the Trek are not social workers. They do not meddle in what has happened during the life of the boys in the past. They deal only with what is happening *here and now*. This is a central point during the Trek: the experiences here and now.

Each three and a half weeks the group is visited by an evaluation team from The Netherlands. The members of the team stay for two days. During this time an evaluator has one talk with each boy. During this talk they evaluate the individual process and the attainment of the individually set goals. The evaluator also assigns some 'homework': little subjects to concentrate on during the next period, for example 'make your own decisions' but also 'think about what you want in your relations with your parents' or 'think about what school you will attend after the trek'.

If one looks at the developments these young people show during the trip, it appears that four phases can be distinguished. Of course the length of these phases cannot be determined precisely and varies among the participants. If all four phases are completed, we conclude that the trip has worked - at least in the short term.

In the first phase, which can be described by the imperative *'Walk, do not talk'*, all the youth's energy goes into the walking itself. Especially at the beginning, when the body has not yet adjusted to heavy physical exertion, the kids must really exert themselves just to reach the day's destination. They ask themselves why they ever agreed to participate ('What the hell am I doing here?'), even when the destination has been reached. Indeed, the muscle pain, the blisters and the welts caused by the heavy backpacks keep the memory of the misery they have just been through alive. One saving factor seems to be that the other participants (including the two leaders) are bearing the same cross. They can all share the pain. But little by little the youths' bodies become accustomed to the difficult physical demands. They begin to develop some self-confidence and hesitantly they build up a feeling of pride.

In phase two ('*Just look at me!*'), most of the grumbling subsides and everyone is surprised by his or her own achievements. Apparently they begin to enjoy the trip. So far they have just barely made it but this cannot squelch the satisfaction they feel. And the nature around them appears to hold something wonderful: some participants even dare to express this feeling aloud.

During this period a crucial breakthrough in the emotional life can take place; the tough shell of armour that kept the expression of feelings suppressed, is now slowly breaking down. When the participants have reached the halfway point in the trip, a psychologically important point has been reached as well: the project is halfway over and they can count the remaining days. So they realize something has to happen because 'before you know it you'll be home again'.

The third phase starts when the participants begin to think about what will happen after the trip. They realize that '*It's got to be different!*', even when the plans for the future are abstract and global and not yet well thought-out. For the time being they only know for certain what it is they do *not* want to happen again: no more fighting with their parents, no more problems with the police, etc.

In the fourth phase, '*What will I do?*', the plans gradually become more concrete and realistic, partially because of the discussions the youngsters have had with the leaders and the members of the evaluation team.

7.4.3 Training of social skills

Then the group returns from Norway and everything seems to have changed. Almost without exception all participants who finish the Trek are filled with positive intentions and they are willing to change their lives in The Netherlands. The Trek, i.e. the positive feelings of having finished something they had to fight for, has increased their self-confidence and self-respect. For most of them it is one of the very few things they have completed in life without failing! Now they are able to look at the future. And they are willing to take their chances.

The positive power the participants return with is rather rough and without direction, but it is also delicate: actually the youngsters are vulnerable. When they try to pick up their lives in The Netherlands there will be disappointments and consequently there is the risk of enormous setbacks to the whole process. It is important that the youngsters' early experiences be favourable as they try to reha-bilitate.

For this reason the group is kept together at a HHK house. There the youngsters get a short but intensive training in social skills (cf. Bartels, 1986; Van der Veer & Slot, 1987; Slot, 1988; Slot, Jagers & Dik, 1990). We try to give them the tools for gaining positive experiences. Most members of the target group of this special assistance project never had the opportunity to learn these skills during their normal upbringing.

During the training the emphasis is on social skills they soon will need in 'normal' life (for example applying for a job, renting a room, resuming contact with their parents, making new friends).

7.4.4 Post Counselling

An integral part of the project is the post counselling period. In developing the program the post counselling period has turned out to be the most crucial part of the project; it seems to be decisive for success or failure. All the positive intentions the youngster returns with from Norway should be realized in The Netherlands, i.e. in Den Haag.

Directly after the training period each juvenile is considered individually in order to determine whether he or she is able to live in a private room or needs some prolonged training in practical and social skills. The intention is to let the youngster live in a private room as soon as possible.

At the beginning of the post counselling period there is daily contact with the participant. Later on the frequency of counselling contacts diminishes gradually. During this post counselling period the staff of trek leaders harks back to the base of the trek itself: directly by reminding the participant of what he/she achieved during the Trek ('You solved huge problems in Norway so now you can solve this tiny one, too'); and indirectly by using the positive feelings and trust that have come about as a result of participating in and completing

the Trek.
At the end of the post counselling period, which lasts about six to nine months, the youngster lives totally independently.

7.5 Some results of the project

The value of any residential treatment program is in the progress the participants make during the program, including maintaining it afterwards. One of the great problems of many residential programs and experiential education projects is the lack of systematic scientific experimental research.
Van den Bergh and Scholte studied the results of one particular HHK Trek in 1986. They concluded that participants showed significantly less aggression and violence, and exhibited less reserved, anxious, restless and dull behaviour after the Trek. The investigation provided an impression of some short-term results of a trek (see also De Vries, Van den Bergh & Scholte, 1986).
We wanted to get a better insight into the way participation in a rather long-lasting survival trek program influences the lives of the juveniles, so we investigated long-term changes in the lives of the participants.
We got in touch with all the youngsters who participated during the first four years of the project. They were interviewed (by questionnaire) from two and six years after they left the program. The response rate was 75%.
Although the results of this investigation are positive, some remarks should be made in advance. We did not use a control group, so we were not able to compare the results with those of other treatment methods. Likewise it is impossible to make a clear distinction between the treatment effects of the program and the normal cognitive and socio-emotional developments which occur during adolescence. Considering the limits of the research design the results can only give us an impression of the facts.

In table 1 some demographic data regarding the sample of 48 former participants is shown. The data reflect the time the juveniles entered the project.

Table 1　　　*Participants in the HHK trek program; demographic data (n = 48)*

Ratio boys : girls	9:1
Average age	17,5
Parents divorced/left/died	72%
Left school without finishing	71%
Average social assistance career (in years)	3,2
Average number of residential settings visited before	2,9

An indication of the behaviourial problems of these participants can be found in the written reports of the social authorities (cf. table 2). Of course more than one problem can be mentioned.

Table 2　　　*Behaviourial problems of participants according to social authorities' reports (n = 48)*

Truancy	69%
Criminality	58%
Aggression and violence	44%
Passivity	42%
Excessive use of drugs	38%
Running away	35%
Drifting lifestyle	33%
Vandalism	21%

The participants in the project were quite problematic youths, had been placed many times in children's homes and institutions and showed different sorts of behaviourial problems. Most of them hardly participated in society. They showed quite a lot of anti-social behaviour and they no longer attended school or worked.
Two to six years after they took part in the project their situation appears to have improved radically (table 3).

98

Table 3   *The situation of former participants, two to six years after leaving the project (n = 48)*

Living situation	
lives on his/her own	56%
lives with parents	25%
lives with others	8%
lives in a residential setting	11%
Goes to school or has a job	72%

From these numbers one can draw the conclusion that many of the participants are in a better position now than before they took part in the program.

The participants seem to agree with this. We asked them if their life had changed since they took part in the program. We got the following answers:
(table 4).

Table 4   *Views of former participants, two to six years after leaving the project (n = 48)*

Perception of actual living situation	
life is better than before	64%
life is just the same as it was before	31%
life is worse than before	5%
Perceived influence of HHK program on living situation	
positive	58%
not positive	11%
I don't know	31%

In indicating how life had changed, the participants not only mentioned that they now have a job, go to school, have a diploma, and successfully live on their own. They also mentioned that they had learned to discover and to know themselves, that they had gained confidence and had developed better relationships with their parents. Furthermore they said they felt happier and were able to continue their relationships with a partner. Finally they mentioned better prospects. It seems that experiential education can be a running start to social competence!

7.6 Working elements

What happens during a survival trek (as a specific example of an experiential education project) to produce the favourable results mentioned above? We assume, based on the literature and our own experience, that the following elements (which can be distinguished but not separated) are collectively responsible for the positive effects of the trek.

One of the most prominent 'working elements' is: *Deprivation*. Extreme conditions lead the participant to many confrontations with 'the self', often many more than an experienced social worker can bring about. Nobody can seclude oneself from the influence of hard circumstances. The name 'survival trek' is not casual: deprived of all luxury the youngsters are faced with the task of completing an extremely strenuous and lengthy trip. They launch a fight with themselves. Winning means strengthening a positive self-image.

Challenge, excitement and adventure are also central elements in this project. As Schouten, Blankstein and Hirsch (1974, p. 63) pointed out, many kids (boys) with anti-social behaviourial patterns need a 'thrill'. They can find this 'thrill' in criminal activities but also in adventurous projects.

How adventurous is modern life for a teenager? Most of it seems predictable, especially to youngsters who have to get along with a small reservoir of capabilities and who have had few chances in life: in their eyes life appears predictable in the negative sense.

The adventure and the possibility of unexpected events stimulates the youngsters to participate and the 'Rambo-like' image of the trek (like a 'struggle for life') encourages them and makes the project attractive; participation in the project is in marked contrast to living in an institution. This attraction is a fruitful starting point for an assistance project. Schouten et al. (1974, p. 64) stress the relation between the need for a thrill and the omnipotence fantasies of adolescents with socio-emotional problems: thrill compensates for failures in everyday life. However, in the project the thrill is directly related to reality: 'Rambo' has got to finish his daily route!

Locus of control. Van der Ploeg (1990) states that many youngsters in residential settings lack the experience of having an influence on their own lives. As a consequence their 'locus of control' is often *external.* Participation in the project offers them an opportunity to turn life around and to be - more than in the past - in command of the situation (a change they have to fight for, day after day).

Nature. The peaceful and impressive experience of being in the countryside makes another important contribution to the whole process. Enjoying nature and indulging in the fine feelings it evokes can be the beginning of giving room to one's own feelings again. For most participants, coming from urban areas, this is a completely new experience.

Isolation. It is also important that the participants are removed from the environment in which they displayed their behaviourial problems. From behaviouristic theories we know that behaviour is very closely related to the situation in which it occurs (Slot et al., 1990). Taking them out of the situation where the problems arose and were reinforced, offers the youngster new chances. Unknown circumstances create a possibility for experimenting with new styles of coping and new behavioral patterns. Amidst the unknown surroundings and the new people with whom they are travelling, they can think about the future without being troubled too much by the past. Reversion to previous behavioral patterns is partially prevented by shielding the young people from the inhabited world during the trek.

The counsellors and the evaluation team. The people who work with the youngsters are crucial. The counsellors contribute to the changes desired in the young people by confirming their newly developed self-confidence, by giving the participants feedback, and by stimulating them to think about what they will do after the trip has been completed. The evaluation team stimulates the process of change by periodically reminding the participants of and convincing them to stick to the agreements they made during the trip and by evaluating the progress made.

7.7   Conclusions

The results of the follow-up study show that a long-lasting survival Trek can be a very effective assistance project. Target groups that can scarcely be reached with more traditional methods, i.e. unmotivated kids with poor chances in life, seem to benefit especially (cf. Binder-hagel, Van Empel & Van der Net, 1992; Van Dijk & Hilhorst, 1992). Considering the group the project is aimed at, the results are surprisingly good. That does not mean that all participants made progress: about 30% did not. The situation became even worse for some of them; they lost their last hope: "If a method this tough does not work for me I must be a hopeless case!"

Experiential education can answer some, but not all of the difficult questions we have to deal with in residential care. Many questions still arise. Are long-lasting projects more effective than short-term projects? Should the experiential education project be the core of a program (comparable with the HHK-project) or should it be just a stimulating element in a residential treatment program? Are experiential education projects only useful for young people with conduct disorders or anti-social behaviour? How severe should the activities be? These and many other questions arise while working with these projects. In conclusion Bartels and Van Gageldonk (1990, p. 101) say that there is a complete lack of systematic evaluation research on experiential education.

So far the development of experiential education projects has been conducted almost exclusively by some private institutions. These projects primarily arose as an alternative to traditional methods in residential care which failed. In combination with the non-intellectual and practical character of a program merely based on activities, this might explain the 'gap' that exists between the scientific world and the world of experiential education.

Although experiential education projects show good prospects for broadening the range of treatment alternatives in (residential) youth care, more systematic research is needed to answer questions such as those asked above. One can not expect private institutions to develop evaluation studies on a broad scale. The universities should take the challenge!

References

Bartels, A.J. (1986). *Sociale vaardigheidstraining voor probleemjongeren.* Lisse: Swets & Zeitlinger.

Bergh, P.M van den, & Scholte, E.M. (1984). *Eindrapport wetenschappelijk onderzoek Overlevingstrektocht.* Den Haag/Leiden: Haagse Hervormde Kindertehuizen/Rijksuniversiteit, Vakgroep Klinische en Orthopedagogiek.

Binderhagel, H.R., Empel, M.W.M. van, & Net, Th.Z.J. van der (1992). *Ervaringsleren; theorie, uitgangspunten en bouwstenen voor het beleid, deel 1.* Tilburg: Instituut Toegepaste Psychologie & Educatie.

Davidson, W.S., Redner, R., Amdur, R.L., & Mitchell, C.M. (1990). *Alternative treatments for troubled youth, the case of diversion from the justice system.* New York: Plenum Press.

Dijk, A.G. van, & Hilhorst, N. (1992). *Leren door ervaring: eindrapportage overall-evaluatie experimenten ervaringsleren in de jeugdhulpverlening.* Amsterdam: Van Dijk, Van Soomeren & Partners.

Een voettrektocht als begeleidingsmiddel (1984). Den Haag: Haagse Hervormde Kindertehuizen (unpublished).

Gageldonk, A. van, & Bartels, A.J. (1990). *Evaluatieonderzoek in de jeugdhulpverlening. Deel 1 en 2.* Leiden: DSWO Press.

Goffman, E. (1961). *Asylums, essays on the social situation of mental patients and other inmates.* New York: Anchor Books.

Helmantel, H. (1991). Ervaringsleren: beginselen, mogelijkheden en toepassing. *Tijdschrift voor Jeugdhulpverlening en Jeugdwerk, 3,* 5, 31-35.

Helmantel, H., & Hilhorst, N. (1991). Invoering ervaringsleren. *Tijdschrift voor Jeugdhulpverlening en Jeugdwerk, 3,* 5, 50-52.

Keulen, T.P. (1991). Ervaringsleren als aanloop naar sociale competentie; jongeren lopen in Scandinavië. *Tijdschrift voor Jeugdhulpverlening en Jeugdwerk, 3,* 5, 36-40.

Kraft, R.J., & Sakofs, M. (1988). *The theory of experiential education.* Boulder (CO): Association for Experiential Education.

Overleven in de asfaltjungle; exploratief onderzoek onder deelnemers aan voettrektochten (1989). Den Haag: Haagse Hervormde Kindertehuizen (unpublished).

Ploeg, J.D. van der (1990). *Gedragsproblemen; ontwikkelingen en risico's.* Alphen aan den Rijn: Samsom.

Prie, H. du (1991). Ervaringsleren als ordeningsinstrument. *Tijdschrift voor Jeugdhulpverlening en Jeugdwerk, 3,* 5, 41-44.

Ruyter, P.A. de (1983). Inrichtingsopvoeding, nee. Residentiële hulpverlening, ja mits. In J. van Weelden, R. de Groot, & H. Menkveld [eds.], *Onvoltooid of onbegonnen? Hulpvragende kinderen I: Antropologische uitgangspunten* (pp. 151-166). Groningen: Wolters-Noordhoff.

Schellevis, P. (1985). *In beweging kun je sturen.* Amsterdam: Stichting voor het Kind.

Schouten, J., Hirsch, S., & Blankstein, H. (1974). *Laat je niet kennen; over residentiële behandeling van adolescenten.* Deventer: Van Loghum Slaterus.

Slot, N.W. (1988). *Residentiële hulp voor jongeren met antisociaal gedrag.* Lisse: Swets & Zeitlinger.

Slot, N.W., Jagers, J.D., & Dik, M. (1990). *Handleiding kursushuismethodiek.* Amsterdam/Duivendrecht: Paedologisch Instituut.

Veer, K. van der, & Slot, N.W. (1987). *Sociale vaardigheidstrainingen als alternatief voor een sanctie.* Amsterdam: Paedologisch Instituut.

Vries, D. de, Bergh, P.M. van den, & Scholte, E.M. (1986). Overlevingstrektocht als begeleidingsmiddel. In W. Hellinckx [ed.], *Kwaliteit in de hulpverlening m.b.t. kinderen met psychosociale problemen* (pp. 225-247). Leuven/Amersfoort: Acco.

Weg, F., & Bliek, W. (1991). Behandeling volgens een aktiviteitenmodel; ervaringsleren bij BJ-internaat De Baanderhoek. *Tijdschrift voor Jeugdhulpverlening en Jeugdwerk, 3,* 5, 46-49.

Zandberg, Tj., & Naayer, P.M.H. (1987). *Kenmerken van kleinschaligheid.* Den Haag: Coördinatiecommissie Wetenschappelijk Onderzoek Kinderbescherming (CWOK).

Ziegenspeck, J. (1990). *Erlebnispädagogik; Rückblick, Bestandaufnahme, Ausblick.* Lüneburg: Klaus Neubauer Verlag.

8 Social Competence Training for Deaf Adolescents with Severe Antisocial Behaviour

N.W. Slot & T. Zandberg

8.1 Introduction

The prevalence of deaf children in the Netherlands is estimated at 2 to 3 in 10.000 (van Dijk, van Eijndhoven, 1990). This means that the total number of deaf minors lies between 800 and 1200. These youths have a total loss of hearing. Thirty percent of the deaf is multiple handicapped.
Apart from the deaf there are youths with a hearing impairment.
A very important factor in terms of development, is the time of onset of deafness. The majority of the deaf children are born deaf; less than a fifth becomes deaf as a result of illness after birth. We speak of pre-lingual deaf children when the child has become deaf before the phase of speech development. In this contribution attention will be focused on this particular group of deaf children.
Deafness severely affects all aspects of development. Communication is a basic problem in education and treatment. Within the field of education of the deaf the advocates of the so-called oral method emphasize the acquirement of language and functional speech. The supporters of the so-called 'total communication approach' recommend the use of sign language together with the use of body language, speech and written language. The underlying idea is that deaf children for whom language and speech are the only way to communicate, will have less opportunities for engaging with their environment. As a result they might drop behind in their development.
Very young deaf children receive care from institutions for the deaf

through home training services. In the Netherlands there are five institutions for the deaf. All of these have a very long history (the oldest is over 200 years old). Three of these institutions also provide residential care.

8.2 The necessity of a 'Working and Living Together'-Project for deaf children with severe antisocial behaviour

Education has always been given priority within the care for the deaf. Initially children were only placed residentially if they had to cover too great a distance to reach school. Nowadays pupils are admitted more often because of complex (behaviourial) problems. The deaf children in residential treatment often come from multi problem families.

A recent study conducted at the residential institution of "H.D. Guyot", showed that 40 percent of the youths came from families with poor relationships. In 20 percent of the families there was a change of parents. For 60 percent of the youths, conduct disorders were are among the indications for referral (Kranenborg, 1991).

In dealing with deaf children and their families the institutions are faced with more problems and more complex problems as well. Consequently there is a growing orientation towards treatment. Since January 1st 1991 these institutions have the official status of a treatment facility.

Most of the deaf children with conduct disorders can be treated in these institutions. Youths with severe conduct disorders however give rise to threatening situations. Lack of personnel, knowledge and means account for the fact that the institutions are unable to offer this specific group adequate treatment. Therefore it was decided to set up a specialized treatment unit. Because the number of these youths is estimated to be low, the capacity of this unit has been restricted to eight places. If necessary a second unit with an equal capacity of eight places will be set up.

In order to set up an effective project, the institutions for the deaf have contacted the Department of Special Education of the University in Groningen and the Paedological Institute in Amsterdam. The former department has been asked to conduct an independent study, focusing on the description and evaluation of the of the main components of the new project, called the 'Working and Living Together project'. The Paedological Institute has been approached for the development and implementation of the treatment programme.

8.3 The Working and Living Together Project: target group, goals and organization

The 'Working and Living Together project' (WLT) offers specialized help to average intelligent pre-lingual deaf youths up to 21 years old with severe conduct disorders.

A youth will be referred to the WLT project when it has become clear that he or she cannot be treated adequately in a residential unit of a common institution for the deaf. On no account should the project become a centre for youths without severe conduct disorders. The objective of the project can be formulated as follows: Social competence training of deaf youths with severe conduct disorders in an integrated living/learning situation. After a stay of approximately two years, the youths should be able to live in one of the regular residential facilities for the deaf or to live independently.

The project started early in 1991. A farm house was bought in Alphen a/d Rijn in the centre of Holland. It was decided to make a quick start because at least four youths needed help urgently. At present, four youths are living in this project, one youth is living independently and receives supervision from the project. The youths are called "kursist" ("Student" or "course member").

The farmhouse is being renovated. When this is completed, accommodation can be provided for eight youths who will all have a bedroom of their own. Beside a number of common rooms, there will be facilities for education and vocational training. The project is easily accessible, also by public transport, for parents and other involved people. Consequently it is possible to maintain the necessary contacts with the surrounding world (of the deaf) and schools (for the deaf).

Effatha, a christian institution for the deaf holds administrative responsibility for the project. The admission committee comprises representatives of the five institutions for the deaf and a consultant youth psychiatrist.

Seven trainers (one of whom is living in with his family), two

regular teachers, one coordinator and one special educator (academic level) are attached to the project. By this formation continuous supervision is guaranteed 24 hours a day. The working and living together project can be characterized as small-scale community-based treatment setting. These settings have the following characteristics (Zandberg, 1991):
- a restricted number of youths and trainers;
- a high degree of autonomy for the trainers regarding the daily responsibilities for the treatment;
- self-supporting in daily care activities (food and clothing, contacts with school, employers and parents).

These characteristics are partly opposed to those of the so called 'total institution' (Goffman, 1961). A small-scale community-based treatment setting offers the advantage of a high degree of continuity and involvement, an individual approach to the youth, a clear structure and organization, less stigmatizing, less aggression and less problems in maintaining order and spontaneous learning of every-day skills (Zandberg, 1991). All these advantages link up with the problems of the target group. Additionally, the concept of community-based treatment fits perfectly with the so called 'social competence model' that has been a leading principle in many projects of the Paedologisch Instituut. (Slot, 1988; Kok, Menkehorst, Naayer, Zandberg, 1991).

8.4   The programme[1]

8.4.1 The basic treatment principle in 'Working and Living Together'
The main goal in the 'Working and Living Together'- project (WLT) is the improvement of social competence.
Social competence is defined as the degree in which a youth's response to tasks arising from everyday social interaction, is evaluated as being adequate. The improvement of social competence can

---

[1] With thanks to Karin van der Zande and Frans Plieger, staff members of the Working and Living Project.

be accomplished in two ways: 1) through social skills training and-/or 2) task alleviation. This model has been supported by different authors. In several studies it was found that youths with antisocial behaviour showed poor social competence. (Patterson, 1982; McFall & Dodge, 1982; Freedman, Donahoe, Rosenthal, Schlundt & McFall, 1981).

Bartels (1986) studied the characteristics of effective treatment programmes for delinquent youths and demonstrated that all these programmes were aimed at teaching concrete everyday skills that enable these youths to function more successfully in society. Bartollas (1985, p. 574) concluded in his review of the literature on juvenile delinquency: "Effective programmes ... help delinquents develop skills that prepare them for adjustment in the community. These range from educational and vocational to interpersonal and problem solving skills". Ross and McKay (1980) showed that the teaching of new skills, instead of emphasizing inappropriate behaviour, is a major characteristic of successful residential treatment programmes.

8.4.2 The Kursushuis: a source of inspiration for 'Living and Working Together'

'Living and Working Together' has been inspired by a programme for youths with antisocial behaviour called Kursushuis. This programme has been developed by researchers of the Paedological Institute in Amsterdam/Duivendrecht. The Kursushuis-programme is based on 'Achievement Place', an American community-based program for antisocial youths. (Braukmann & Wolf, 1987). Achievement Place has been adapted for mentally retarded adults (Sherman, Sheldon, Morris, & Strouse (1984) as well as for autistic youths (McClannahan, Krantz, McGee & MacDuff, 1984).

The programme includes three main components: 1) the motivation system: a series of token systems through which a youth proceeds, 2) teaching, the use of training techniques based on instruction and modelling and 3) 'semi-selfgovernment', partial responsibility for the youths in planning the programme. Outcome research indicates that the Kursushuis programme is effective. Six months after completing the programme, former Kursushuis youths show significant improvement in many aspects of social competence and show less delinquent behaviour than during the pre-treatment period (Slot, 1988; Slot, Jagers & Beumer, 1992).

During the initial preparations for the development of 'Working and Living Together' the Kursushuis researchers were invited to join the project-team. As a result, 'Working and Living Together' incorporates many components of the Kursushuis programme.

8.4.3 Assessment and teaching in 'Working and Living Together'

In the 'Working and Living Together' project the social competence of each youth is being assessed in three ways:
- assessment of social competence in six domains,
- a task-skill analysis of inappropriate behaviour,
- a functional analysis of inappropriate behaviour,

The six domains of social competence include:
- Communication. This domain includes total communication: sign language, oral communication, finger spelling etcetera and the use of 'visicom': a telecommunication system for the deaf.
- Independent living. Including: personal hygiene and health, cooking, cleaning, handling money, shopping, doing the laundry etc.
- Vocational and academic achievement.
- Contacts and relationships with peers and adults.
- Daily life. This domain includes skills and tasks related to daily life in and outside the project. Examples are: travelling, keeping track of time, planning a day.
- Leisure time.

For each youth an initial assessment of social competence is being made during the first weeks of his or her stay in the programme. This is carried out through careful observation of a youth's response to all tasks that are part of the daily routine. For this reason, each domain of social competence is represented in the daily routine.

A second approach in assessing social competence is a task-skill analysis of inappropriate behaviour. Conduct disorders and antisocial behaviour are predominant problems for each youth referred to WLT. Within a social competence frame of reference these problems are considered inadequate responses to tasks. The first step in an analysis of inappropriate behaviour is a task analysis. The question is: which tasks are involved? The second step is the selection of skills that may suit the tasks involved. A third approach is a functional analysis. This procedure focuses on the 'learning history' regarding the problem behaviour. Which circumstances typically cause the problem behaviour? Is the problem behaviour being reinforced? What sort of reinforcers are involved?

Assessment is done repeatedly. Each assessment results in a 'working and teaching plan' comprising the goals for the next weeks.

Teaching includes all the techniques and procedures used to improve social competence. We differentiate between: positive feedback, training by instruction and training by modelling.

Positive feedback is an essential technique in WLT. It is given each time when a youth gives an adequate response to a task during the daily routine of the project. Positive feedback proves to be a difficult technique for trainers. There are several reasons for this.

Firstly this technique requires constant alertness of the trainers. Positive feedback is more effective when it is applied immediately following the adequate behaviour. This is true for hearing youths but is especially important for the deaf. In a programme for hearing youths a trainer might say: "Ann that reminds me, you did a terrific job this morning when you packed your schoolbag. You thought of everything you needed for school today". Theoretically speaking, a trainer might convey the same message to a deaf youth. But in practice it proves to be difficult to communicate frequently about events in the past.

A second reason why positive feedback is difficult is related to a problem-oriented attitude of many trainers. Problem behaviour is spotted more easily than positive behaviour. This does not mean that trainers have a negative approach towards their job and the youths. Living together with youths with severe conduct disorders simply is so strenuous that it proves difficult to notice positive behaviour. There are two mechanisms that serve as reinforcers for the use of positive feedback by trainers. One is frequent feedback by the coordinator and the special educator. The second mechanism is the effectiveness of this technique. Trainers experience that positive feedback 'works'. Even if a trainer is upset or angry, the use of positive feedback proves to be far more effective than negative feedback or punishment.

Because positive feedback is so important, a token reinforcement system has been developed that not only enhances the use of feedback but also the youth's response to feedback. Each youth entering the WLT starts at level one of this system. During the day the youth earns and loses points on his token card. Each domain of social competence is represented on the card.

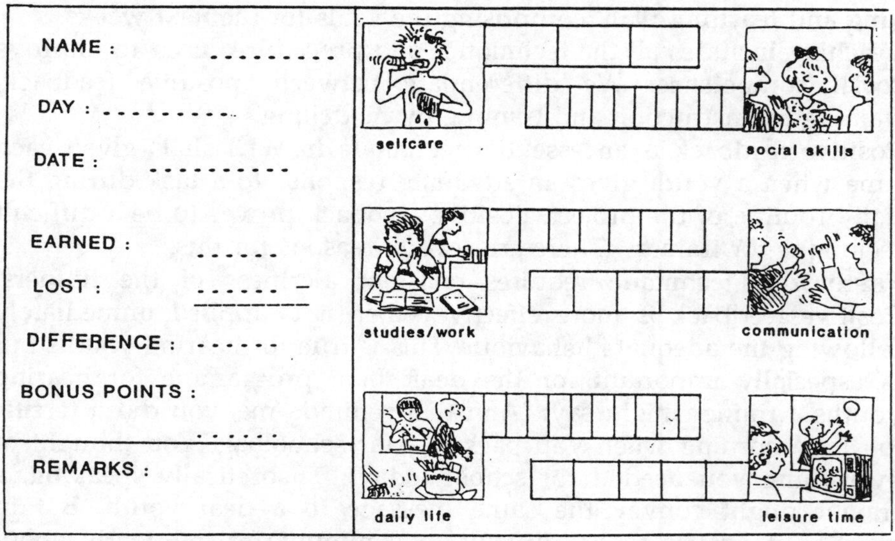

Figure 1   Pointcard

At the end of the day the daily difference between points earned and lost is calculated. Depending on the daily difference the youth earns privileges for the next day. Examples of privileges are: the use of special games, extra free time etcetera. Since the trainer focuses mainly on positive feedback, the youths earn their privileges quite easily. If the daily difference exceeds a certain amount of points, the extra points are put on an 'account'. As soon as the youth has acquired a certain amount of these extra points he or she proceeds to the next level of the token system. At present there are four levels in the WLT token system. As the level goes up, the system becomes more and more individualized. At the same time more emphasis is placed on written information. Sometimes individual adaptations of the token system are needed, for example when a youths shows very problematic behaviour. In that case an hourly, or even a 30 minute system is enforced.

Training by instruction is the teaching of a skill or the transfer of information in a structured way. This technique is a component of the Kursushuis programme and has been adapted for the deaf. It is important that training by instruction is applied each time a youth is engaged in a task requiring a new skill or new information. Not only does the trainer have to employ this technique in a proper, non confronting way, but he or she also has to recognize the moments during the daily routine that are suitable for training.

Training by modelling is used when oral instruction together with sign language is not sufficient. The best way to learn how to use a lawnmower is watching somebody who gives explanations and shows how to use it. Different models are used during training by modelling. Models can be trainers, but also therapists or teachers during individual or group skill training. Youths who have proceeded to higher levels of the programme may serve as models for youths in an early stage of the programme.

Although the main focus is on teaching of new behaviour, attention has also to be paid to inadequate, negative behaviour since all youths in the WLT have a history of conduct disorders. The trainers use different techniques for stopping inappropriate behaviour. An essential component of these techniques is a description of alternative behaviour. It is not sufficient to tell (or to sign) a youth that he has to stop doing something. It is crucial to tell the youth what he or she might do instead.

8.4.4 Living together in a community-based programme
Different from what happens in a Kursushuis, the trainers do not live together with the youths. However, this principle is not entirely abandoned. On the premises, next to the farm house, a couple lives with two small children. The husband is a fulltime trainer in the WLT. The WLT-youths have frequent contacts with all members of this 'neighbour-family'.

The daily routine in the project is strictly scheduled. Individual youths or small number of youths engage in several activities in the field of communication, independent living, vocational and academic achievement, contacts and relationships with peers and adults, daily life and leisure time. The WLT is certified by the government as a special school.

Apart from these activities each youth has one or more household

responsibilities. Each day the youths and the trainers on duty participate in the daily conference. They discuss the current topics in the
programme, the fairness and usefulness of rules, the planning of an
outdoor activity, etcetera.
The youths, trainers and the neighbour-family are in frequent contacts with the community. Some youths for example have part-time
jobs. Parents of the youths are regularly invited to the WLT project.
On the basis of the recent working and teaching plans the progress
of their son or daughter is evaluated. Visitors are always welcome in
the project. A visit is an excellent opportunity for the youths to show
the visitor around and to explain the programme.
The development of the above described programme started in the
spring of 1991. The research has started six months later. The goals
of the research and some preliminary findings will be highlighted in
the last two sections.

8.5 The study

The study concerns a description, analysis and evaluation of the
above described WLT programme. Considering the lack of a well
described and well-tested treatment programmes for this target
group, it will be necessary to give a detailed description of the
project as well as the process of program development.
At the first stage of the evaluation study, attention will be focused
on the need for this specific treatment service. The following issues
will be described and analyzed:
- The planning and decision making process at the start of the
  project.
- The measures that are necessary to realize the formulated plans
  and a description of the conditions that are required to offer the
  intended help.
- The transition from initial plans to the actual programme. Ample
  attention will be paid to intermediate adaptations.
- Characteristics and demands for help of the youths admitted.
- Treatment goals and treatment procedures.
- Characteristics, properties and skills of the professionals/teachers.
- External factors, for example: influence of the neighbourhood,
  referring agencies and collaboration among the participant orga-

nizations.

Next, the research results should provide information on the criteria for indication, admission and discharge of the youths. It should be made clear which diagnostic techniques can be used to formulate adequately the demand for help of the deaf youths with conduct disorders.
Furthermore, the study should provide insight regarding the conditions for an optimal and stimulating climate the programme.
Finally the description and evaluation of the treatment programme are to contribute towards the quality of treatment of the deaf with conduct disorders in the five existing regular institutions for the deaf.
For the study a policy model will be applied as developed by Mayer and Greenwood (1980). For the Dutch residential youth care this model has been further elaborated by Mesman Schultz, Depla and Nelen (1987).
The study is characterized by the three following activities:
a Theoretical insight by means of a review of the literature and interviews with experts.
b Questioning and observation of the practice of the daily care. Not only are the actual activities important, but also the professionals' motivations.
c Practical testing of tentatively formulated strategies within the programme of the target group under controlled conditions. Characteristic of the testing will be case studies and N=1 studies (Barlow and Hersen, 1984).

In phases a and b qualitative research techniques and (sometimes participating) observation will generally be used.
At this stage, the formulation and development of variables and strategies in the programme are of particular interest. When the programme has won enough confidence, the first testing can take place in phase c. The results of the study should answer the question whether the developed treatment programme in phases affects the formulated goals of the experimental project in a positive way.

8.6   Tentative results and conclusions

The WLT project has been set up in a place where it is well possible to realize community-based treatment. In practice it appears that the residents are indeed able to maintain contacts with their environment. Some residents make use of the educational facilities of the regular institutions for the deaf.

All trainers, the coordinator and the special educator have been trained in the basic components of the treatment model.

In future the coordinator and the special educator will take care of this training themselves. In addition, all staff-members have followed a course of sign language. The next step was the development of a daily routine. This was done by the coordinator and the special educator together with the Paedological Institute. Subsequently the phases of the treatment programme have been defined and individualized observation logs and treatment plans have been introduced. Each youth has his own working-scheme and pointcard.

Every youth shows progress in the six domains of social competence, although there are considerable differences among them. This conclusion is based upon the competence ratings by trainers. The first results will be published at the end of this year (1992).

Apart from positive developments there are also problematic factors.
- For professionals who were trained in the regular institutions for the deaf it appears to be difficult to work within a strict elaborated treatment programme.
- A number of trainers have pulled out in the meantime for various reasons.
- The WLT is still too greatly obstructed by organizational structures of the institution to which it is attached. This makes it difficult to be flexible and self-supporting.
- The planned rebuilding of the farm house causes much unrest.

In spite of the (sometimes great) difficulties it appears that the treatment programme improves the functioning of the participant youths. The youths are positive about their programme. As one youth said: "I'm learning to trust myself".

References

Barlow, D.H. & Hersen, M. (1984). *Single Case Experimental Designs.* New York: Pergamon.

Bartels, A.A.J. (1986). *Sociale vaardigheidstraining voor probleemjongeren.* Lisse: Swets & Zeitlinger.

Bartollas, C. (1985). *Juvenile Delinquency.* New York: John Wiley.

Braukmann, C.J. & Wolf M.M. (1987). Behaviorally Based Group Homes for Juvenile Offenders. In: E.K. Morris & C.J. Braukmann (Eds.) *Behavioral Approaches to Crime and Delinquency.* New York: Plenum Press.

Dijk, J.P.M. van & Eijndhoven, J.J.M. van (1990). Recente ontwikkelingen in de dovenpedagogiek: controversen en meningen. In: *Handboek Orthopedagogiek*, 4171, (pp. 1-16). Groningen: Wolters-Noordhof.

Freedman, B.J., Rosenthal, L., Donahoe, C.P., Schlundt, D.G. & McFall, R.M. (1978). A Social-Behavioral Analysis of Skill Deficits in Delinquent an Nondelinquent Adolescent oys. *Journal of Consulting and Clinical Psychology, 46,* 6, 1448-1462.

Goffman, E. (1961). *Asylums. Essays on the social situation of mental patients and other inmates.* Harmondsworth: Penguin Books.

Kranenborg, A. (1991). *Opname, altijd raak? Een onderzoek naar opnamecriteria voor het Internaat voor Doven 'H.D. Guyot'.* Doctoraalscriptie. Groningen: Rijksuniversiteit, Vakgroep Orthopedagogiek.

Kok, J.M., Menkehorst, G.A.B.M., Naayer, P.M.H. & Zandberg, Tj. (1991). *Residentieel Gedragstherapeutisch Behandelingsprogramma.* Assen: Dekker & van de Vegt.

McClannahan, L.E., Krantz, P.J., McGee, G.G. & MacDuff, G.S. (1984). Teaching-Family Model for autistic children. In: U.P. Christian, G.T. Hannah & T.J. Glahn (Eds.) *Programming effective human services: Strategies for institutional change and client transition.* New York: Plenum Press.

McFall, R.D. (1982). A Review and Reformulation of the Concept of Social Skills. *Behavioral Assessment, 4,* 1-33.

McFall, R.M. & Dodge, K.A. (1982). Self-management and interperso-

118

nal skills learning. In: P. Karoly & F.H. Kanfer (Eds.) *Self-management and Behaviour Change*. New York: Pergamon Press.

Mayer, R.R. & E. Greenwood (1980). *The design of social policy research*. Englewood Cliffs: Prentice Hall.

Mesman Schultz, K., Depla, M. & Nelen, M. (1987). *De ontwikkeling van een evaluatie-instrument ter ondersteuning van instellingsbeleid*. Leiden: Rijksuniversiteit, LISBON.

Patterson, G.R. (1982). *Coercive Family Process*. Eugene OR: Castalia

Sherman, J.A., Sheldon, J.B., Morris, K., Strouse, M. & Reese, R.M. (1984). A community-Based Residential Program for Mentally Retarded Adults: An Adaptation of the Teaching Family Model. In C. Paine, G.T. Bellamy & B. Wilcox (Eds.) *Human services that work*. Baltimore: Brookes.

Slot, N.W. (1988). *Residentiële hulp voor jongeren met antisociaal gedrag*. Lisse: Swets & Zeitlinger.

Slot, N.W., Jagers, J.D. & Beumer, M.H. (1991). *Tien jaar Kursushuis: ervaringen en follow-up gegevens*. Amsterdam/Duivendrecht: Paedologisch Instituut.

Zandberg, Tj. (1991). Community based treatment in group homes for youths with social problem behaviour. In W. Hellinckx, E. Broekaert, A. Vanden Berge & M. Colton (Eds.) *Innovations in Residential Care* (pp. 79-94). Leuven/Amersfoort: Acco.

Zandberg, Tj. (1991). Prävention von Verhaltensstörungen in drei Kategorien kleiner Heime. In H. Neukäter (Ed.) *Verhaltensstörungen verhindern* (pp. 236-245). Oldenburg: Universität Oldenburg, Zentrum für pädagogische Berufspraxis.

9 Family-oriented Treatment in a Residential Institute for Adolescent Girls

H. Verzaal

9.1 Introduction

Op Dreef is a small residential institute in Amsterdam for girls between the ages of 14 and 18.

The girls are referred by several out-patient institutes or by a juvenile judge. They have serious problems, usually defined as extreme 'behavioral problems' and cannot stay at home.

In this chapter, the development of a residential institute will be presented, one that has fully integrated the principles of family therapy and theory (Kempler, 1984) into its structure and where family therapy functions as a major component. Family-oriented treatment does not mean the hospitalization of whole families. It means the application of a family therapeutic approach and an interpersonal system concept to the treatment of hospitalized girls from the time of their referral and admission to the time of their discharge. The conviction that family-oriented treatment is indispensable for residential children serves as a basis for the organization of the structure and policy of the whole institute (Verzaal, 1991). Op Dreef has based its policy on this philosophy. Each member of the resident staff has his own specific role in and responsibility for the treatment of the girl and her family. The principles of 'experiential family therapy' (Kempler), have emphasized the methodical abilities of the resident staff members and also determine the ability to involve the families. The institute does not work with natural parents only. Other people who are important to the girl may also be involved in the treatment, for instance step-parents, foster-parents, grandparents, but also friends or other relatives.

9.2 The staff of the institute

The staff consists of a director who is a family therapist and 7 residential staff members (social workers): 4 women and 3 men. This team is jointly responsible for policy development for the institute. In working with families and adolescent girls, new discoveries are continuously being made. Every new experience contributes to a renovation of the policy.

This is a dynamic, never-ending process. In this way, the executers are the makers of the policy and vice versa. The treatment and the treatment planning are carried out by the entire team. In this setting the team discovered that working with the girl's entire family is very important. These are also the people, who, based on practical experience have discovered that "family therapy" is more than an auxiliary therapy, as is the case in most other institutes.

9.3 Family therapy as a frame of reference for the organization

Based on past experiences, the staff discovered that it might be more effective if family therapy were integrated into the whole institutional structure and policy. This means integration of family therapy into the referral of the girls, the admission procedure and the decision to admit, but also into the group work, the individual approaches of the staff with the girls and, last but not least, into staff policy.

Since 1987 we have been working structurally in this direction. The following discoveries have been made:

a)   Since then the length of stay of the girls has decreased considerably. In 1987, the average stay was about 18 months, in 1990 it had decreased to 10 months, and in 1991 to 9.3 months. This development has continued as the staff has become more skilled in working with families.

b)   There is another reason that the girls' length of stay in the institute has decreased: parents and children have been stimulated from the beginning to explore their problems together and to take responsibility for their own situation.

c) Not only does the length of stay decrease. This kind of treatment is also more effective and durable, because parents and children cope with their problems together. No longer must either party cope with their feelings of guilt, anger and sorrow separately (Anderson, 1977; Verzaal, 1991).

d) Another discovery of the staff was the importance of contacting the parents from the outset, meaning immediately after the telephone call of the referent.

In the past, this was much more arbitrary. For example, the referent might suggest that it would be unwise to share the admission procedure with the parents together with the children because this would increase the stress between the family members; or the staff might be told that the parents preferred to be left alone for a while. In such cases we often gave up the attempt to approach the parents directly.

But soon it became evident that we could not cope with the girl's problems. We could not deal with the problematic relation between the child and her parents. We could listen to and interpret the feelings of the girl, but that did not lead to an essential change of behaviour. Then we discussed this with the girl and proposed to her that we invite the parents after all, often weeks or even months after the admission. And how did the parents react in that case? 'You can forget your family talks. You were clever enough to make decisions about our child without our input before, so now you can just figure it out yourself.'

The staff increasingly experienced how much time was lost solving this problem before the real problem could be treated. These experiences finally led to the current procedure, which is to contact the parents immediately after referral in every case.

9.3.1 Working with referral agencies

The referent is asked:
- how the family situation is,
- whether the parents have been informed of this referral and what their feelings are,

- if they are willing to cope with the treatment,
- the kind of treatment used before and why it didn't succeed.

The referent is asked to invite the family for a first visit to the institute.

Should the referent be unwilling, we ask permission to do this on our own.

We find this important for the following reasons:

a) In spite of the problems, parents and children always have a fundamental desire to be together, even if this desire appears to have completely 'disappeared' (Bouwkamp, 1989).

b) Parents always remain responsible for their children, though they may no longer be capable of taking that responsibility. This means that the staff cannot assume this responsibility from the parents, but instead must help them one way or another to again assume this responsibility themselves (De la Marche, 1983). Experience shows that parents want nothing more than that, but because of feelings such as disappointment, frustration, anger, shame and so on, they can no longer cope. Their attention has long been diverted from this desire to take responsibility and has shifted to blaming the child: 'that is the child with problematic behaviour', the problem child. Often the parents feel, rightly or wrongly, that they are bad parents (Bouwkamp, 1989). Parents often tell about how they have felt rejected and stigmatized by social workers before. They felt attacked and misunderstood in their inability and they stopped the therapy prematurely. Is hospitalization of the child then the final solution? Answering this question now would be premature.

c) In most families of children with problematic behaviour there are also authority problems. Often the bigger the authority problem the bigger the behaviour problems (Van Acker, 1988). That is another important reason to involve the family in the treatment.

9.4   The admission procedure

9.4.1 The acquaintance meeting
Parents and children are invited for an acquaintance meeting. For the parents and the children it is important to meet the staff members, to see what they can expect and to hear what the staff expects of them. They have to know these things before they can decide to start the admission procedure.

9.4.2 The admission meeting
The admission policy of the institute is that the parents decide on the admission, and not the staff (Byng-Hall & Bruggen, 1974; De la Marche, 1983). During this admission meeting we look for the potential of each individual for change instead of endless discussions about what went wrong and why this happened (Kempler 1984). It is important that this first meeting *not* be limited to gathering information about the child. "Questioning merely puts the family on the defensive, ignores their needs and establishes a totally patient-oriented contract" (Anderson, 1977). Attention must be paid to what they have been going through, to their needs, and to their feelings about their child being in the institute. In order to formulate realistic goals with a family, the focus is on:
a)   the behaviour that prevents the family and the child from working together without our support.
b)   the behaviour and attitude that are especially upsetting to each person,
c)   what changes each person would like to have.

It is the staff's responsibility to assist the family to specify their needs and desires since such goals as 'better communication' or 'a happier life' are too general to help give direction to treatment. The staff members can facilitate establishing mutually agreeable treatment goals by sharing their own perceptions and feelings about what they see and their additional recommendations for goals with the family.

The purpose of the admission must be clear to everyone and it must offer hope, because as soon as the family members have some perspective of their situation, they are willing to co-operate (Anderson,

124

1977). Therefore, during the admission phase, we together make a plan with therapeutic points. Family therapy sessions, as well as the stay in the group and the individual contacts between staff members and girls must support the achievement of these goals. For some girls this plan means that they will return home as soon as possible. Others prefer to work towards an independent life. However, the family members decide what is desirable and possible for them. The main focus is: work towards a better relationship among the family members. From that position good choices can be made.

9.4.3 Clinical application: underlying concepts
In working with families the staff has been inspired by the experiential approach of Walter Kempler. In this approach, the following questions are essential:
- How will the parents react?
- As a social worker what do you expect from the first contact with parents?
- What is your objective?
- What kind of things do you expect to encounter?
  (Kempler, 1984).
Very often, the staff is confronted with parents who are resistant because of fear, discomfort and misunderstanding. In addition, parents usually do not ask for hospitalization of their child (Harbin, 1979). Their first reaction to the invitation will be:
'Shit, here we go again, we'll be called to account again'. They will protect themselves from that however they can. It is important to break through those mechanisms of resistance, for instance:
1. by meeting the parents openly, without prejudice, (which might have arisen based on the reports made by the referral agency, which is read by the staff member prior to the first meeting);
2. by understanding their resistance and especially by telling them that: 'it is understandable that you are not willing to deal with us. However, we ask for your involvement, because we need
· you. We cannot help your child without your information. You know your daughter best, you know what has already been tried, how successful it was, what went wrong.'

After making a lot of mistakes, we discovered that this first meeting or the first telephone call with the parents is the most difficult contact. But it determines the direction of further treatment. This contact is crucial for their cooperation. In training this first contact is emphasized so that the residential staff members become aware of the moments where they feel that they lack skills, in the face of escalating discordant interactions. By exploring those moments, we learn that this feeling of ineffectiveness has more to do with ourselves than with the client at the other end of the telephone line. The way clients behave can stir up memories of unfinished family business for a staff member, and can make it hard to be supportive to these families (Anderson, 1977). Personal resistance emerges as a reaction to the way the parent approaches the resident worker. This resistance prevents an open relationship from being established with the other person. Exploring such resistances and experimenting with other behaviour helps to free ourselves from those resistances, and makes us feel free to meet the parents openly and directly. Learn to be personal, dwell on what you see and hear and what it does to you, and do not be afraid to share those feelings with the family - members. Confront people straightforwardly with what you see missing in their way of interacting and how sad you feel about that. Or say what feels good to you to reinforce that behaviour (Verzaal, 1991).

9.5   The policy of the institute

It is important for the staff members to have insight into their own ways of interacting. It takes more to be a good therapist than knowledge of theoretical issues and strategies alone. The therapist should not think that he must have the solution to every problem or that he is the only wise person in the world. Attitudes like these paralyse clients and confirm their feelings of failure, guilt and shame. It does not encourage them to co-operate in thinking about how to manage the problems in their family. Much more effective would be to ask the parents for their help. Our experience is that it can be a revelation for parents and children to hear the therapist say that he does not know how to go on and that he needs their help. After all, as well as being a therapist, you are a human being like them, with similar desires and needs. You, too, experienced ups and downs in your upbringing (Verzaal, 1991).

This theme is a hot item in the team of Op Dreef. You don't have to look far to find it. Look around the team. How do team members behave with one another? We can draw a parallel towards every family interaction. How much space do we give one another to be ourselves in the context of the team? Part of the team does the talking, while the rest grows silent. How dare we pretend to have therapeutic skills for coping with disturbed interaction patterns, when we cannot deal with them among our colleagues. Insufficient insight into our own way of functioning does not lead to change in our own behaviour or in that of our clients. The patterns that we recognize in ourselves are the same as those we carry with us in our contacts in the adolescent group and in the family therapy sessions (Letulle, 1979; Verzaal, 1991).

9.5.1 Contra-indication for admission
If the staff does not find openings into a family system, this might be a contra-indication for admission. Such situations can also occur during treatment - moments at which the therapist feels that he lacks the skills needed to continue treatment. It is, of course, very tempting to accuse the family of this breakdown - saying, for example, that the parents beg off, or that they are not keeping the agreements made at the beginning or that the daughter refuses to open up, etc. All those explanations might be true, but the question is what does the staff do next? The decision not to admit or to terminate an admission can be made quickly. We have discovered that it is more honest to discuss our own limits. We ask ourselves why we are not making progress in this situation, with this particular family or with this girl. Relevant questions are:
- Why and especially where do we become ineffective?
- What makes that happen?
- Why do the parents not co-operate any more?
- What have we done or not done, which has caused the parents to lose their motivation to co-operate with us?
- Where have we deserted them?
- What could create new openings?

During the weekly staff meeting much time is devoted to finding answers for those questions. In addition, inter-vision meetings are used to explore these items and to train staff regarding them. In some cases supervision of the Kempler Institute is requested, either with or without a particular family.

9.5.2 *The staff policy*
New colleagues are not asked to have all these therapeutic skills. But we do emphasize their willingness to develop these relations with other people, which means with the colleagues and clients. In other words: 'is there a willingness to open yourself up to another and to learn from these experiences?' So the most important question is: 'Who are you?' instead of 'What are you?'.

The staff members in the institute have been completely integrated into the family therapy.

That is a choice motivated by the desire to prevent a break between what happens in the family therapy sessions and the attention given in the group. This choice was made in light of past experience, when it was not a matter of policy that staff members dealt with family therapy. Several problems arose, for example, rivalry and competition between parents and staff members. Problems of loyalty between staff members and the hospitalized child on the one hand, and between parents and their child on the other hand, occurred frequently (Mandelbaum,1972; Harbin, 1979; Wiewouters et al, 1982; De la Marche, 1983).

Of course, they have not completely disappeared, but they are now recognized much earlier and are working points in the therapy sessions.

An example: A girl asks a staff member if she is allowed to go out in the evening and to return much later than normally allowed. If the staff member agrees, the girl tells her parents during a visit that William (a staff member) says that she can come home at two o'clock at night (though the parents say she can't). This issue leads to a struggle between parents and the staff member. The staff has discovered that it is much better to stimulate the girl to learn to negotiate with her parents about what she wants. Particularly during the therapy sessions, and of course with the help of the therapist. By making these desires therapeutic points, the family members learn to negotiate with each other to reach a decision which satisfies everyone.

9.5.3 *The organization structure*
This working method has been determined by the organizational

structure of the institute.

It is expressed in two principles:

First, we do not believe in the myth that knowledge is restricted to the specialists and that their knowledge is superior to the knowledge of people on the work floor.

Such an idea leads to a gap between the specialist and the practical workers, in this case the staff members. In addition, treating colleagues this way has a very discouraging influence on the people who do most of the work with the girls and their parents (Van den Dungen, 1992).

Second, the small scale of the institute contributes to fulfilling these principles of methodology.

There are direct communication lines among the colleagues, which make it possible to develop a common frame of reference. The institute becomes a coherent system, so that family members encounter the same way of thinking and working in all their dealings with the institute.

References

Acker, J. van (1988). *Ouders en kinderen in conflict*. Deventer: Van Loghum Slaterus.

Anderson, C.M. (1977). Family intervention with severely disturbed inpatients. *Arch. Gen. Psychiatry*, *34*, 697-702.

Bouwkamp, R. (1989). Het monsterverbond. In S. de Vries [red], *Wat wij ik noemen*. Batenburg: De Overdracht.

Bouwkamp, S. (1989). Taak en persoon van de therapeut. In S. de Vries [red], *Wat wij ik noemen*. Batenburg: De Overdracht.

Byng-Hall, J., & Bruggen, P. (1974). Family admission decisions as a therapeutic tool, *Family Process*, *13*, 443-459.

Van den Dungen, M.G.M. (1992). Jeugdhulpverlening, wetenschap en beleid; een driehoeksverhouding. *Tijdschrift voor Orthopedagogiek Kinderpsychiatrie en Klinische Kinderpsychologie*, *17*, 1, 3-19.

Harbin, T.H. (1979). A Family-Oriented Psychiatrice Inpatient Unit. *Family Process*, *18*, 281-290.

Kempler, W. (1984). *Over experiëntiële gezinstherapie*. Deventer: Van Loghum Slaterus.

Letulle, L.J. (1979). Family therapy in a residential treatment for children. *Social Work, 24*, 49-51.

Mandelbaum, A. (1972). Parent-Child Separation. It's Significance to Parents. In G.H. Weber & B.J. Haberlein (Eds.), *Residential Treatment of Emotionally Disturbed Children* (pp. 68-83). New York: Behaviour Publications.

Marche, J. De la (1983). Hulpverlenen..niet overnemen. Een gezinstherapeutische residentiële behandelingsunit voor jonge adolescenten. In S. Verhaest & R.A. Pierloot (Eds.), *Vastgelopen jeugd...laatste kans* (pp. 185-217). Deventer: Van Loghum Slaterus.

Verzaal, H. (1991). *Niet uit huis zonder thuis*. Amsterdam: Vereniging Beth San.

Wiewouters, C., De Vriendt, A. & Pyck, K. (1982). Tussen conflict en samenspraak: over de interaktie tussen groepsopvoeder en ouders binnen een residentiële setting. *Tijdschrift voor Orthopedagogiek, Kinderpsychiatrie en Klinische Kinderpschologie, 7, 2*, 80-91.

10 The Guidance of Youngsters in Halfway Homes regarding Problems with their Parents

M. Klomp

10.1 Introduction

For a long time the relation between youngsters in halfway homes and their parents has been neglected. Recently this situation has changed (De Korte & Poeze, 1985; Vink, 1986). In many halfway homes much more attention is being paid to the problems youngsters have with their parents. The way youngsters are guided in this respect varies. However, a clear methodical framework is lacking. The purpose of this article is to contribute to the development of methodical approaches to the guidance of youngsters related to problems with their parents.

We deal with the following subjects:
- Recent developments in halfway homes (2).
- Problems that youngsters have in their relationships with their parents and allied goals of guidance (3).
- Different settings for guidance (4).
- Methodical principles (5).

The discussion of these topics is based upon inductive research into methods of counselling in halfway homes. In this study 12 counsellors in 7 halfway homes were followed for half a year. The study involved the guidance of 31 youngsters (Klomp, 1992). Furthermore, we will refer to the results of a national survey of the general characteristics of halfway homes in The Netherlands. 94% of all halfway homes participated in this national survey. It involved 175 halfway homes with a total of 1179 youngsters.

10.2 Recent developments in halfway homes

A halfway home is an ordinary, relatively large house in a residential area where four to eight youngsters with behavioral problems live. Each person has his own room; the kitchen and bathroom are shared. The youngsters go to school or are employed. They have to do their own cooking and cleaning. In other words, they are more or less self-supporting. They are guided in the way they live by counsellors. This guidance has treatment as well as training aspects.

Until recently the attention halfway homes paid to youngster's problems with their parents was minor. 'We take the side of the youngster. This means that we only get involved with the problems he has with his parents if he wants us to do so. Loyalty to the youngster is an important issue...' This is the kind of statement which one could frequently hear made by a counselor at that time in a halfway home. Some counsellors also referred to individual responsibility and to the youngster's growing up process. Different circumstances led to such an attitude among counsellors:

- Most of the youngsters in halfway homes came from residential care. Their family background was vague.
- The halfway home represented an interim stage for the youngsters between residential care and independent living. There was a focus on practical living problems.
- The geographical distance between the halfway home and the parent's residence was often large.
- Financially the youngster was relatively independent of his parents.

Since the beginning of the Eighties there has been a change in these circumstances. An explosive growth in small-scale forms of residential youth care has occurred. An interim stage between residential care and independent living is no longer necessary. The preparation of the youngsters for independent living takes place in the small-scale residential unit itself. Halfway homes have become an alternative for residential care instead of an interim stage. This has two consequences:

* Youngsters who are admitted to halfway homes often show

serious psycho-social problems. As a consequence, the focus in halfway homes has changed from 'practical training' to 'treatment of psycho-social problems'.
* More and more youngsters in halfway homes come directly from a (foster) family. The national survey in halfway homes shows that 57% of the youngsters come directly from a (foster) family whereas 38% of the youngsters come from residential care. Consequently a discordant family background is frequently encountered.

As a result of the economic recession youngsters have become financially more dependent on their parents. Regionalisation also plays an important role. Youngsters in halfway homes are living closer to their parental home.

These developments have given the attention to parents an explicit place in the organizational structure and the working procedure of halfway homes.

10.3 Problems of youngsters in relation to their parents and allied goals of guidance

Problems of youngsters in halfway homes in relation to their parents are more apparent than before, as explained in the former paragraph. First we will work out the relationship between the problems of the youngster and the family situation. Then we will look at the goals of guidance which can be inferred from this.

10.3.1 *The relationship between youngsters' problems and the family situation*

The connection between youngsters' problems and the family situation can be observed on three different levels.

Family problems
From literature about the functioning of families (a.o. Vuyk, 1986; Jansma, 1988) we know that problems within the family such as emotional neglect, scapegoat mechanisms, parental divorce, traumatic experiences such as incest, the death of a parent, and so on, influence the behaviour of the children. Youngsters in halfway homes are characterized by such family backgrounds. The national survey in

halfway homes reveals the following results.

Table 1 Situation of the parents of youngsters in halfway homes.

	parental divorce	married or living together	one/both parents died	unmarried mother	other	total
number (n)	502	277	107	28	4	918
number (%)	55	30	12	3	0	100
unknown or not recorded						261

70% of the youngsters in halfway homes live in a one-parent family of one sort or another. Many of these youngsters have been confronted with different (and changing) step-parents.

De Wit and Van der Veer (1984) observe that in recent decades the family has assumed a more explicit role in children's emotional development. Many families of youngsters in halfway homes fail in this area especially. There is an insufficient basis of warmth and safety, which is needed by youngsters to face new situations. In other words: the basis for experimentation - having a sense of safety - is lacking. Youngsters in halfway homes often face the world outside full of mistrust.

Moreover family problems can lead to problems in the identity development of the youngster, because of the lack of acceptable identification models within the family. This can result in a negative identity.

In adolescence youngsters with long-term residential experience, where their own family has faded into the background, often show a renewed interest in their past. Delfos (1977) writes about these youngsters: 'The youngster will want to investigate his life history. Questions like 'Who is my father?' and 'How is my sister getting along?' arise. Understanding his own life history is very important for the youngster. It contributes to the development of his self-image and identity. It gives him something to hold on to in his search for perspective. A real step toward independence often requires dealing with a vague and only partially known past.

Learned dysfunctional behaviour
The family is the place where the youngster gets his first experience in developing social relations; he learns to deal with people. There is a connection between the child-rearing style of the parents and the family culture. The process of socialization within the family has been described by Stapf, ed. (1972) and by Geene (1976). In this context the research of Geurts and Tesser (1976) is interesting. They studied the subcultural aspects of so-called 'working-class-families'. These families are characterized by a inability to influence their own situation, little participation in social life, and opinions which are based on tradition rather than their own choice. Geurts and Tesser (p.124, 143) specify these characteristics as follows:
- A strong emphasis on obedience. Relations are defined in terms of power: a nice child is an obedient child.
- The division of tasks in the family has been determined very strictly. There is a clear difference between male and female roles.
- Feelings of powerlessness within the family cause the children's motivation for achievement to be poorly developed.
- The nature of work (if there is any work) is often uninteresting and boring. An intrinsic motivation for work does not count for much; financial reward is more important.
- The attitude of the family members is passive and is oriented to the immediate satisfaction of needs.
In other words there is very little stimulation for experimentation.
What can occur in these families is that youngsters accept and incorporate the values of their family without ever questioning them. In fact this is a matter of premature identity formation or so-called 'identity foreclosure' (Marcia, 1980).
Behavioral problems of youngsters have a complex background, in which temperament and education as well as socialization play an important role. The youngster learns specific behavioral patterns within the family. This behaviour is persistent, because the youngster is familiar with it. Research has shown that the behavioral patterns the youngster learned within the family are repeated after the youngster enters residential care (Blankstein, 1971). These learned behavioral patterns are so powerful that group leaders in residential care can hardly resist them and tend to behave like the parents did. One of the goals of residential care, according to Schouten, Hirsch and Blankstein (1974, p.104), is: 'to release the youngster from the

136

doom of the past'.
Behavioral patterns which the youngster has learned in the family
can be observed in halfway homes as well (Klomp, 1987). On one
hand this behavior gets the youngster into trouble; on the other it is
familiar to him. Giving it up causes uncertainty and the feeling that
he is not safe. Moreover the dysfunctional behavior is often supported by parents and friends.

The parent-adolescent crisis
In the attempt to establish their identity, youngsters question the
norms and ideologies of their parents. The youngster increasingly
makes his own decisions and develops his own lifestyle. The transition from secure family life to the unknown world of life as an adult,
involves a change in family interactions. The youngster may be
opposed to his parents and authority conflicts may arise. This causes
a 'developmental crisis' within the family (Schoorl, 1981, p.44). Many
youngsters in halfway homes have similar problems with their
parents. There is too much negative communication between them:
quarrelling, mutual disqualification and so on. The parents no longer
know what to do and the youngster feels rejected. The negative
spiral that may arise has been analyzed by Van Acker (1983) and by
De Wit and Van der Veer (1984). The latter devote attention to the
risk of the development of a 'negative identity', which means an
identity based on identifications and roles, which can be considered
unwanted and dangerous. An example of this is the youngster of
decent, proscriptive parents who joins a violent gang.
For youngsters from ethnic minorities, who represent a large part
(19%) of the population of halfway homes, the process of establishing
new patterns of authority and interaction is very complex. In the
Islamic culture, for example, being an adult means feeling responsible for the fortune of one's family, subjugating oneself to family
traditions and respecting the prevailing norms and values. This is
opposite to norms and values such as independence and self-respon-
sibility, which are generally accepted in western European countries.
The admission of a youngster to a halfway home itself can cause a
split between the youngster and his family which can be difficult to
mend.

10.3.2 *Goals of guidance*

The general goal of halfway homes is: 'the enhancement of practical, psycho-social and social self-reliance and independence of youngsters as individuals'. The activities undertaken by the parents are derived from this general goal. The specific goals of guidance follow naturally from the request for help, expressed in the behaviour of the youngster (Kok, 1991). On the basis of the relationship between problems of youngsters and the family situation - as elaborated in paragraph 3.1 - the following 'requests-expressed-in-behaviour' can be mentioned:

a 'Help me to develop a better way of dealing with people, so I will no longer be dependent on the dysfunctional ways I learned within my family.'
   This can be threatening to parents. It is a confrontation to their own dysfunctional ways of dealing with people.
b 'Help me to communicate with my parents in a positive way. We only see the negative aspects of each other as demonstrated by the many quarrels we have had and still have. Help me to recognize the good things in my relationship with my parents.'
   The parents do not know how to deal with the behaviour of the youngster and feel powerless. They experience his behaviour as negative. The youngster feels rejected by his parents. Thus a vicious circle of mutual rejection and disqualification arises. One of the targets of the counsellor is to help both parents and youngster to break out of this vicious circle.
c 'Help me to develop a more equal relationship with my parents. My parents think they know what I should do. They still treat me like a child. Help me to have an open mind about the things they say and stimulate me to make my own decisions about it. Teach me how to negotiate with my parents.'
   The process of growing up often involves authority conflicts. The counsellor has to stimulate the youngster and his parents to consider each other as equal partners (see a.o. Van Acker, 1983).
d 'Help me to deal with past negative experiences so that they do not influence the way I behave so much. Teach me to see my parents as they (also) are in spite of these negative experiences.'
   Several youngsters are weighed down with traumatic experiences such as sexual abuse or maltreatment. These experiences negatively affect their way of dealing with parents or with other people.

e 'Help me to recover who I am and what I want. In this my parents play an important role, because they gave birth to me. Help me to discover the significance of my parents in relation to who I am.'
Youngsters with a vague family background may search for their roots. Other youngsters have identification problems with their parents.

10.4 Different settings for guidance

The goals of guidance elaborated in paragraph three are basic to the guidance of youngsters regarding problems with their parents. Starting from this frame of reference the counsellor is able to influence the interaction between youngsters and parents in different ways, directly as well as indirectly. In a former study (Klomp, 1986) we analyzed the different settings in which guidance activities deal with problems between youngsters and parents took place. The most frequently occurring situations for guidance were:

10.4.1 Formal contacts between the halfway home and the parents
In cases where the youngster volunteers for a halfway home, the parents continue to be formally responsible for their child. They have to agree to the youngster's stay in the halfway home and they have the authority to end this stay. Consequently there are formal contacts between the halfway home and the parents. One of the first possibilities for contact is the informative meeting at the beginning of the halfway home period. During that meeting parents are told about the working procedure in the halfway home. Furthermore there are periodical evaluation meetings, where important decisions sometimes have to be made about the future of the youngster. Formal contacts are favourable for other contacts. The parents have been in the halfway home, they have been informed and they are acquainted with the counsellor. The counsellor has a first impression of the youngster's parents. Those first contacts make later contacts in case of problems easier. Moreover, when parents have improper prejudices about the halfway home, these prejudices can be removed early on.
The formal contacts are also a confirmation of the respect of the

halfway home for parental responsibility. This enhances the 'psychological accessibility' of the halfway home for the parents.

10.4.2 Informal contacts between the counsellor, the youngster and the parents

Contacts between the youngster and his family will be stimulated, unless there is a reason to stop this contact temporarily. Sometimes the counsellor will participate in these contacts. They give him the opportunity to see how youngsters and parents communicate with each other. This information makes the counsellor less dependent on the youngster's stories about his contacts with his parents. Moreover, the counsellor is able to intervene in the interaction between the youngster and his parents. He can also show the youngster how he could deal with specific reactions of his parents in a different way (modelling). In these contacts the attitude of the counsellor towards the parents is very important. The research of Wiewauters (1982) in a child psychiatric clinic showed that parents are very sensitive to this attitude. The way the counsellor introduces himself, talks about the youngster, presents himself - all these things are interpreted by parents in a positive or negative way.

10.4.3 Counselling activities with the youngster

The counsellor has regular (at least once a week) conversations with the youngster to discuss his functioning in and outside the halfway home. In these sessions the youngster's problems with his parents can be discussed. The counsellor does not wait until the youngster brings something up, but initiates these discussions as well.

In addition to these organized counselling sessions there will be all-day contacts between the counsellor and the youngster. This involves talks while drinking coffee or washing dishes. The atmosphere is more informal. Both the youngsters and the counsellors can put out feelers. Each one can see how the other reacts. These all-day contacts can provide themes for the counselling sessions.

However, it should be emphasized that even without talking about the parents, the counsellor expresses something about them in his behaviour toward the youngster. De Vriendt & Wiewauters (1985) call this 'indirect contact with the parents via the youngster'. Examples are: ignoring the parents, forming a coalition with the youngster against the parents, and so on. The attitude of the counsellor is always an influential factor in the contacts between the young-ster and his parents.

10.4.4 Intervention contacts with the youngster and his parents
Now and then there are planned sessions between the counsellor, the youngster and his parents. The themes of these sessions differ: a conflict between the youngster and his parents, things that the youngster does not dare to discuss with his parents by himself and so on. There are one or more planned sessions about a specific theme and with a clear purpose. Sometimes other people (such as a super-visor) participate in these sessions. This is especially true if the parents consider the counsellor prejudiced, for instance in a situation of conflict.

This type of intervention contact most often occurs when communi-cation between the youngster and his parents has come to a stand-still.

10.5 Methodical principles

The way the counsellor intervenes during the different guidance situations is very important. A lot depends on his attitude toward parents and youngsters. Rivalry and loyalty problems occur easily. The counsellor has to deal with the different interests of parents and youngsters. It is not easy to remain objective and to be acceptable to both parties. The study of methods of guidance in halfway homes, mentioned in the introduction has resulted in a number of methodi-cal principles that are useful for the counsellor.

10.5.1 Joining
The relationship between the youngster and his parents often has a history of discord. The parents are frequently sceptical about the admission of the youngster to a halfway home. Feelings of rivalry may arise against the counsellor. Therefore an open, inviting attitude is very important. Parents should be respected as parents. The counsellor takes both what the youngster and his parents say seri-ously and he avoids passing judgement. He asks for information, shows recognition and tries to fit in with the manners of the family.

10.5.2 Varying support
In the process of growing up, authority conflicts with the parents normally occur. Both the youngster and his parents will try to claim the support of the counsellor to strengthen their own position in the conflict. The involvement of the counsellor with the youngster can easily lead to 'over-identification' with the youngster. However 'taking the side of the youngster' does not imply 'sharing the view of the youngster'. This would only confirm the youngster in his opposition to the parents. The counsellor has to encourage the youngster and his parents to establish new patterns of authority and interaction.
Varying support of the youngster and his parents keeps both involved in the process and helps them to find a new balance.

10.5.3 Staying out of the conflict
The counsellor has to stay out of the conflict. He should not take sides nor should he assume responsibility for the solution of the conflict. This would make it impossible for him to guide the youngster and his parents in the process. The youngster and his parents have to be confronted constantly with their own responsibility for solving their problems.

10.5.4 Relabelling
In a conflict situation the behaviour of the 'opposite party' is generally interpreted negatively. When a boy is seen by his parents as a 'troublemaker', anything he does will be interpreted from that context. 'Having his own opinion' is easily interpreted by parents as 'he is making trouble again'. By the same token a youngster who constantly feels under inspection by his parents, will interpret any form of involvement as inspection.
It is important that the counsellor be able to change the interpretation of such situations for the better. In 'inspection' there is an element of 'concern and interest' as well. In this way youngsters and parents learn to look at each other in a more positive way. In doing so both can break out of the vicious circle of negative communication.

10.5.5 Enhancement of positive interactions
In case of a constant quarrel between the youngster and his parents,

the interaction will be restricted to the on-going problems. When talking about problems, new problems arise. There will be an excess of negative communication. The youngster and his parents constantly put each other down. Positive aspects which may exist are no longer seen. The counsellor has the difficult task of enhancing positive interactions. The youngster and his parents are stimulated to undertake pleasant activities together. Or they temporarily get a banning order on discussing problems with each other.

The counsellor gives them tasks that lead to positive interactions. These tasks have to meet three criteria:
- they must be achievable;
- they must be concrete;
- they must produce results quickly.

10.5.6 Reality testing
In the problems of interaction between parents and youngsters feelings of rejection and yearning for acceptance and confirmation play an important role. As a consequence the youngster has high hopes regarding his relations with his parents. A vicious circle can easily arise:

feeling rejected - yearning for acceptance and confirmation - wishful thinking and unrealistic expectations - confirmation and/or conflict - disappointment and feeling rejected.

The counsellor asks the youngster to check his unrealistic expectations: 'Do you think you can change your father?' 'Is it realistic to consider your mother as your best friend?' The ideas the youngster has are persistent. Therefore it is important to have the youngster confront reality for himself.

10.5.7 Enhancement of role-empathy
Persons involved in a conflict are usually trying to strengthen their own position instead of trying to solve the problem. Consequently they are very much pre-occupied with themselves. They stop noticing what the problem means to the other party, what the motives underlying the other's behaviour are. To enhance better understanding, the counsellor will encourage both youngsters and parents to imagine themselves in the other's position. When the youngster can imagine why his parents react in a specific way (and vice versa), a basis for open communication can arise so that the problems really

can be solved.

10.5.8 Encouraging a more equal relationship
The process of growing up involves the search for new patterns of interaction and authority between the youngster and the parents. The counsellor encourages each to consider the other as an equal partner. He tries to stimulate this by:
- talking to parents and youngsters as responsible people;
- reducing mutual involvement;
- creating possibilities for the youngster to develop his own way of life;
- having parents and the youngster negotiate with each other.

10.6 Conclusion

The relationship between youngsters and parents in halfway homes is complex. The problems of the youngsters are related to the family situation. Often there is a background of discord. As a result of a developmental crisis in adolescence authority conflicts may arise. Guiding youngsters through these problems is a difficult task for the counsellor. The eight methodical principles elaborated in this article are an attempt to develop a methodical approach for counsellors. Basic to this approach is the attitude of the counsellor toward youngsters as well as parents.

References

Acker, J. van (1983). *Adolescent en gezin; conflicten samen oplossen.* Deventer: Van Loghum Slaterus.

Blankstein, J.H. (1971). *Herhaling van gezins-relatiepatronen in een behandelingstehuis.* Rotterdam: Bronder Offset.

Delfos, M. (1977). *Begeleid wonen als therapeutisch instrument.* Utrecht (ongepubliceerd).

Geene, H. (1976). *Het gezin: de appel en de boom.* Nijmegen: Dekker & Van de Vegt.

Geurts, J. & Tesser, P. (1976). *Werkende jongeren en hun onderwijs.*

Nijmegen: Link.

Jansma, J.B.M. (1988). *Gezinsklimaat*. Utrecht: Rijksuniversiteit, Vakgroep Kinderstudies.

Klomp, M. (1986). Aandacht voor oudercontacten in trainingscentra voor kamerbewoning. *Tijdschrift voor Jeugdhulpverlening, 14*, 19-25.

Klomp, M. (1987). Methodiekontwikkeling in trainingscentra voor kamerbewoning. *Tijdschrift voor Orthopedagogiek, Kinderpsychiatrie en Klinische Kinderpsychologie, 12*, 23-31.

Klomp, M. (1992). *Hulpverlening aan adolescenten; een bijdrage aan methodiekontwikkeling in trainingscentra voor kamerbewoning*. Leiden: vakgroep Orthopedagogiek (dissertation).

Kok, J.F.W. (1991). *Specifiek opvoeden*. Leuven/Amersfoort: Acco.

Korte, P. de & Poeze, M. (1985). *Op zoek naar de sleutel voor oudercontacten*. Utrecht: Rijksuniversiteit, Vakgroep Orthopedagogiek.

Marcia, J.E. (1980). Identity in adolescence. In J. Adelson (ed.) *Handbook of adolescent psychology* (pp.159-187). New York: Wiley.

Schoorl, P.M. (1981). *Het gezin in opvoedkundig perspectief*. Lisse: Swets & Zeitlinger.

Schouten, J., Hirsch, S. & Blankstein, H. (1974). *Laat je niet kennen*. Deventer: Van Loghum Slaterus.

Stapf, K., Hermann, Th., Stapf, A. & Stäcker, K.H. (1972) *Psychologie des elterlichen Erziehung*. Stuttgart: Klett.

Vink, W. (1986). Oudercontacten in het wooncentrum. In *Verslag studiedag trainingscentra kamerbewoning voor jongeren* (pp.36-46). Utrecht: WIJN.

Vriendt, A. de & Wiewauters, C. (1985). De interactie 'groepsopvoeder - ouder' nader bekeken. In A. de Vriendt, J. de la Marche & K. Pyck (red.) *Groepsopvoeders en ouders; tegenstanders of medestanders?* (pp.75-97). Leuven/Amersfoort: Acco.

Vuyk, R. (1986). *Opgroeien onder moeilijke gezinsomstandigheden*. Leuven/Amersfoort: Acco.

Wiewauters, C. (1982). *Mogelijkheden en grenzen van de interactie tussen groepsopvoeder en ouders binnen een residentiële setting*. Leuven: Katholieke Universiteit, vakgroep Kinderpsychiatrie.

Wit, J. de & Veer, G. van der (1984). *Psychologie van de adolescentie*. Nijkerk: Intro.

11 Crisis in a Residential Home, a Case Study

P. Durning

11.1 Introduction

This research into an important crisis in a residential home, is part of study conducted in France in the mid-eighties, in order to shed light on the links between relations among the staff and the effects on the children living in residential settings. The general purpose is to study the educational processes regarding children brought up outside their families based on a psycho-sociological approach focusing on links between relations, organizational processes and foster parenting in collective settings.

The theoretical frame includes studies of the social climate in groups and organizations and was developed in the thirties (Mayo, 1933). It was developed and enriched by themes derived from psychoanalysis (Jaques, 1951; Lvy 1969; Enriquez, 1972). A second group of references deals with the studies conducted in therapeutic communities (Goffman, 1968; Racamier, 1973; Rapoport, 1974) and finally, specific studies of the social climate in residential settings (Redl, 1972; Moos, 1975; Tremblay, 1976). We should note that the effects of climate and special disturbances are more serious in child care settings than in the normal industrial organi-zation. In a factory a bad climate decreases productivity. In child care, it changes not only the quantity but even the nature of the educational task.

We initiated these studies by examining critical incidents, thinking that they could reveal very important psycho-sociological pheno-mena. In my doctoral thesis (Durning, 1978), I studied the effects of a theft in a residential setting. The results showed that this caused a lot of trouble among the staff teams, especially since the thief remained unknown. Critical incidents are interesting and are frequently used in qualitative approaches. The study of such incidents is easier because they act as lapsus or parapraxis in a psychoanalytical perspective which allow for the reconstruction of a situation in its integrity and complexity.

At the end of this research, a large study was conducted in which five residential homes were observed over a period of one year. Thus it was possible to observe many incidents, conflicts and major crises. Crises are important to observe in parallel with a systematic approach of ordinary processes (Durning, 1986) especially because of their effects on staff burn-out or on institutional child abuse: violence towards the inmates is particularly likely during these periods. These studies were conducted with a qualitative approach (Bogdan & Taylor, 1975; Pourtois & Desmet, 1988) combining choices inspired by ethnology and periods of field observations. They also included systematic use of a diary. Careful attention was paid to the relations between investigator and subjects, especially when taking into account the incidence of the researcher's presence on the phenomena observed (Devereux, 1980). We also used psycho-social instruments such as interviews and group observations.

In a former contribution (Durning, 1991), I attempted to explain our conceptual frame for understanding the social climate. Here I will present a clinical study.

11.2   Context and methods

11.2.1 Context

The setting studied is a quite important home in the suburbs of Paris, accommodating one hundred children with psychological and behaviourial problems. The staff team also comprises one hundred people.

The home is split into two units. One is called 'the Castle'. It houses 60 children - boys aged 6 to 13 and girls aged 6 to 18. Boys aged 13 to 18 live in group houses in the park. Our study will only deal with the first unit called 'the Castle'. There is a school in the home, which means that there is not only a social staff (group workers) but that there are also school teachers, who, in France, are appointed by the

state. The relationship between school and social staff is often difficult: there are different salaries, holidays, hierarchical organizations,
etc.   -
In fact there are three different teams in this home:
- a medical team with psychiatrists and psychologists;
- a school with teachers and a head-master;
- the educators who do the residential work.

11.2.2 Data collection

We observed this home for one year from February to February,
rather than from September to June - the regular school year - so as
not to miss the important changes from July to September. We were
present every week at the group workers' staff meeting, and had
individual interviews with all the staff at least once, and more often
with the managers. We also had interviews with the children.
During this study we worked on four different sorts of data, which I
shall list briefly.
We studied *texts written by people from the home* concerning the pedagogical projects; two notes written by the senior worker for his team,
one of which summed up all the thefts, runaways and other problems during the critical period with which we were concerned. We
made *audio tapes of the staff meetings* all year long. We also taped the
interviews with staff members (a few of these were conducted during
this period) and *interviews with 17 children* conducted three months
before the crisis. We can also refer to the *diary* in which my colleague
Dominique Fablet and I wrote down our observations, reflections,
questions, etc. every day.

11.2.3 First overview

What leads us to believe we were observing a serious crisis? We
define (operationally) a crisis as a moment of overthrow not limited
to a conflict inside a restricted part of the organization. The crisis can
be identified by exceptional occurrences: unscheduled meetings,
exclusions, dismissals, urgent calls to outside parties (police, judges).
These parties declared the period during and after this time to be
critical as well.
A short empirical description shows a quite special period in November. The researchers were in the home beginning in February
and observed many conflicts between then and June. Many unskilled

group workers left in June or July and were replaced. In August, the staff was on holiday and the children were either with their parents or in summer camps. When we came back in September, much of the educational team (15 people) had been replaced. The manager insisted that it was now a new team, with a new atmosphere and new educational practices. Although the conflicts among educators were very obvious before the holidays, the relationship within the workers' group in September was quite cohesive.

Ten weeks later many children were running away: 11 of the 60 boys left the home, were brought back and left again. There were many other serious difficulties. One month later, the climate seemed far better. The global assessment made by the group was that the term had been quite good.

I believe that we went through a sudden and really violent disturbance. Our research showed important consequences of such a crisis:
- the staff could not focus on their work;
- the effects on the children were serious: anxiety, violence, run-aways.

This study was conducted with two approaches. First, I will attempt to make a chronological description and in the second part I will present the results of a 'cross-sectional' approach.

11.3 Chronological description of the crisis

We will distinguish six periods some of which were very short:
a At the end of August and the beginning of September just after the holidays, the workers were almost all new and unskilled. The most senior had come in the Spring, five months before. They were now working together on a week-end shift from Friday evening to Sunday evening so that they could not meet the other staff members.

The senior worker wanted to start 'on a new basis', as he said; therefore he asked for written group projects and new time tables. These texts were prepared by untrained workers who virtually copied an old text insisting on control, order, cleanliness and so on. The relations in the workers' group were very cohesive and even warm according to the two researchers either attending the meetings or listening to the tapes. This was quite different from what had been observed two months earlier (many conflicts within the former team and between staff members and the senior worker).

One week later at the second meeting, we learned that all the children had been punished on September 17th, because of trouble and noise while changing shoes for slippers in a small corridor before having dinner. Residential workers did not disagree with this group punishment and they remained strongly cohesive. The senior worker said during the meeting: "Children must learn that injustice cannot be avoided in group homes".

b The following week slippers were stolen (when a child could not find his slippers, he was punished). There were more and more punishments. Because a theft had been committed, children were punished every evening for one week. After dinner, the staff forced them to stand without moving until the thief gave himself up. The relations between the members of the workers' team continued to be cohesive.

c In the beginning of October, there was an obvious conflict between the weekend workers' team and the main team over punishment.

For three weeks, we did not hear anything about the children during the meetings but then, at the end of October, we learned that some children were breaking adult's car windows, stealing from private staff rooms and breaking many windows in the home. The parents were asked to pay for the repairs of windows and doors. Conflicts in the workers' team were increasing, especially regarding group punishment. One worker stuck a big poster on his room door which read: "Police! stop violence against children".

d On October 22nd, at the end of the staff meeting, to the surprise of the researchers, and probably of all the staff as well, the senior worker made a long speech explaining that he was taking matters into his own hands. They were now in a state of emergency and he would give the orders.

The following Monday, the dining rooms would be redistributed: the girls would eat in a separate room. He also decided that children should decorate their rooms during their free time.

The team was very depressed; we observed little discussion after the speech of the coordinator and that only from female workers.

Their male colleagues told them "the senior worker trusted us but we failed, so now we must return to a more authoritative style".

e After a short holiday (no school) without any major problems came a few very difficult days. Between November 14th and November 16th eight children aged 9 to 13, ran away a total of 19 times, breaking into and stealing from neighbours' houses. They were brought back by the police but sometimes ran away again a few minutes later.

The level of excitement was very high. Some children believed the head-master had been fired; the whole home was in an uproar. Three children were expelled from the home for three days, which was very unusual.

Team meetings were held daily and went on late into the evening. One female worker had a nervous breakdown. There was a lot of punishment and it was obvious that serious violence was being perpetrated against some children.

f A month later, at Christmas, the global group assessment was good. The team and managers were quite happy that the crisis was over and almost forgotten.

The following section presents a cross-sectional analysis. There are four levels.

11.4   A cross-sectional perspective of the crisis

11.4.1 Adult/child relationship
The first perspective deals with adult/child relationships.
Figure 1 shows that children take initiatives and adults
respond with punishment creating fresh aggression and stronger punishment, etc.
The staff did not try to break the cycle. One must remember however that they had very little training. For instance, the first incident could have indicated the need for a change in the way that children entered the dining room, rather than the need for punishment. Sixty children walking through a small room to change their shoes before eating may explain the mess in the antechamber. Punishment became more and more severe and inappropriate creating a vicious circle.

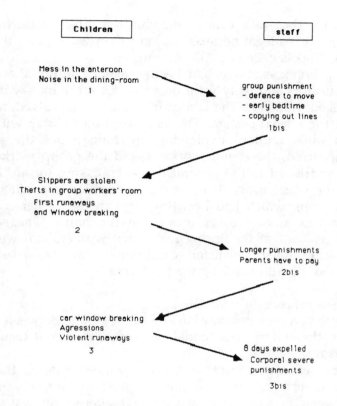

Figure 1   Conflict relations between children and staff

11.4.2   Relations in the group-workers' team

Remember that in September we observed very cohesive relations in the conflicts between the main team and the week-end team.

Later in November, we observed conflicts in the main team. The position of the women was obviously difficult. Many depressing remarks were made during the meetings. At this point, we can digress briefly to look at the impact of preceding events in such settings.

In French residential homes there is a special system called 'transfer' during school holidays. All the children move together with the staff for approximately a week. Young staff can be temporarily recruited for a holiday period from outside the home. Generally the staff is paid more when they take care of the children full-time during the holiday period. It is illegal because the staff then work more than 50 hours a week. This is called an 'illegal transfer'.

During spring holidays, there had been a major conflict about this issue. The educators suddenly went on strike for more money during the Easter 'illegal transfer'. The labour inspector got involved, and of course asked for a legal system. The staff went on holiday with less money. This time, without explaining anything about the events which had occurred, the senior worker asked the group workers to sign a letter addressed to the general manager, asking for an 'illegal transfer' on the usual basis. This, of course, created a conflict with the weekend team, which had been involved in the earlier conflict, and disagreement among other groups in the home. The service workers told us "look at the Spring residential workers that went on strike because of 'illegal transfer' conditions. Now the education team has signed a petition asking for the former system".

11.4.3 Relations between different teams

The third level involves observations of the relations between different teams in the setting: residential workers, the school team and the medical team.

In September, there was a fresh start. New workers ignored the past conflicts and their boss talked about cooperation, non-hierarchical relations between groups, and insisted that everything was to be organized. In September, two interesting points were raised:
- an educator replaced a school teacher for one month, although these categories never cooperated;
- the workers asked for group case meetings with the medical and school teams, although before the holidays residential workers rarely attended case meetings even though it was requested.

Other groups, especially doctors, continued as usual:
- they suddenly arbitrarily took back a room used by residential workers, pretending they needed it;
- the individual case meeting continued as before;
- when the medical team was asked to help at the beginning of the difficult period, they did not participate.

After ten weeks, the same mutual perceptions of hostility and the

usual stereotypes had returned:
- the school made things difficult for the children;
- the doctors lost their influence; they were purely and simply ignored.

11.4.4 Relations within the management team

A fourth level, the attitude of the managers with respect to the institutional conflicts was observed. At the same period, the administrative board modified the relations between the school head-master and chief educator.

Prior to this, they were both second in the hierarchy, which means that when the general manager was absent, the head-master replaced him during school hours and the senior residential worker replaced him at night and during the weekends.

The administrative board, in competition with the school for political position, wanted to move the chief educator up to second position and the head master down to third position in the hierarchy. This proposal was made at the end of October and was rejected by the end of November.

This acute crisis can be analyzed at four different levels. This is not coincidental and explains why the crisis was so serious.

11.5 Short conclusions

In this observation, we must keep in mind the following points:
- the staff was untrained;
- the management was inefficient;
- the staff's conception of residential educational tasks was very poor and therapeutic aims were unclear.

In this study, we had the opportunity to observe the genesis of conflicts and crisis. We can compare this home to the army. The members of the residential staff work for one or two years. They are just like conscripts called for Military Service, without any possibility of changing the attitude of the professional soldiers (chiefs, doctors and teachers).

The following question may be raised: are these phenomena specific to France? Would we find similar crises in northern cultures? In response, it should be noted that I observed similar phenomena in two residential homes in the French-speaking part of Canada (Quebec). Therefore, it seems relevant to study social climate in residential settings in a cross-cultural perspective.

References

Bogdan, R. & Taylor, S.J. (1975). *Introduction to qualitative research methods; a phenomenological approach to the social sciences.* New York: John Wiley and Sons.

Devereux, G. (1980). *De l'angoisse à la methode dans les sciences du comportement.* Paris: Flammarion.

Durning, P. (1978). *Vols à l'internat: approche psycho-sociologique de l'éducation résidentielle.* Thèse de 3ème cycle. Paris: Université de Paris X Nanterre.

Durning, P. (1986). *Education et suppléance familiale; psycho-sociologique de l'internat 'spécialisé.* Paris: CTNERHI (diffusion PUF).

Durning, P. [ed.] (1988). *Education familiale, panorama des recherches internationales.* Paris: Matrice.

Durning, P. (1991). A psychological approach to foster-parenting in residential care. In W. Hellinckx, E. Broekaert, A. Vanden Berge & M. Colton [eds.], *Innovations in residential care* (pp. 227-235). Leuven: Acco.

Enriquez, E. (1972). Imaginaire social, refoulement et répression dans les organisations. *Connexions, 3,* 65-95.

Goffman, E. (1968). *Asiles.* Paris: Minuit.

Jaques, E. (1955). Social system as a defence against persecutory and depressive anxiety. In: *New directions in psychoanalysis.* London: Tavistock.

Jaques, E. (1972). *Intervention et changement dans l'entreprise.* Paris: Dunod.

Lvy, A. (1969). *Les paradoxes de la liberté dans un hôpital psychiatrique.* Paris: Epi.

Mayo, E. (1933). *The human problems of an industrial civilization.* New York.

Moos, R. (1975). *Evaluating correctional and community settings.* New York: John Wiley and Sons.

Pierret, L. (1988). *Les cueils du changement librateur en éducation*. Thèse de 3ème cycle. Paris: Université de Paris VIII.

Pourtois, J.P. & Desmet, H. (1988). *Epistémologie et instrumentation en sciences humaines*. Bruxelles: Mardaga.

Racamier, P.C. (1973). *Le psychanalyste sans divan*. Paris: Payot.

Rapoport, R.N. (1974). *La communauté thérapeutique*. Paris: Maspro.

Redl, F. (1972). The phenomena of contagion and shock effect. In: *When we deal with children* (pp. 197-213). New York: The Free Press.

Tremblay, R. (1976). *A psycho-educational study of juvenile delinquents during residential treatment*. Thesis. London: University of London, Faculty of Education, Department of Child Development & Educational Psychology.

12 Support Issues and Coping Mechanisms in Residential Staff

D.G. Challender

12.1 Introduction

The purpose of this contribution is to explore some of the issues concerning staff survival in residential child care agencies and relates to work in this field by the author who acts as a staff consultant to several agencies in England. It is argued that the social climate of a therapeutic residential community relates to the well-being of the staff and that whatever coping behaviour operates in the staff will inevitably influence the social environment which is created for the residents. Residential care in England is undergoing many changes as a result of changes in legislation and social policy. These developments are creating a situation in which managers of residential establishments need to consider very carefully approaches to recruiting and sustaining high quality staff. This contribution considers the issues and suggests a model for staff support which balances staff needs with those of the residents.

12.2 Residential care in England

There is a pressing need in England to seek answers to many of the questions which confront residential agencies. It is probably well-known that there have recently been several national scandals regarding residential care including the now notorious 'Pindown' regime in Staffordshire. These shocking incidents have occurred at a time when new legislation regarding children (The Children Act,

1989) is being implemented and which has far-reaching implications for children in care - particularly in seeking to protect their rights and in ensuring well-regulated and purposeful residential provision. In this contribution I am setting out to ask a few basic questions regarding residential staff in England. These are as follows:

- Who are the residential staff?
- How do these staff experience their work?
- Are many staff experiencing 'burn-out'?
- What are the coping mechanisms employed by staff?
- What are their sources of support?
- What are the implications of answers to these questions in terms of providing staff support?

12.3 Characteristics of residential staff

One contemporary source of information regarding this aspect is the Report 'Children in the Public Care' (1991) written by Sir William Utting at the request of the U.K. Government following the 'Pin-down' scandal referred to earlier. It is of interest to note some of his observations:

"The whole system of residential care depends upon the commitment and ability of it's staff (the majority of them - historically - young women) many of whom are poorly prepared by training for the job they do....It is unquestionably wearing and responsible work....With residential care widely regarded as a placement of last resort, staff are said - not unreasonably - to be in a low state of morale. At the same time, every exploration of residential child care, every piece of research, every inspection continues to unearth examples of excellent practice....A major problem is simply that residential care of children is commonly regarded as an unimportant residual activity....Thinking about it today is still dominated by historical attitudes towards looking after children - as women's work in which skills are inherent or intuitive and the commitment of the workforce is exploitable."
(Utting, 1991)

Utting's Report points to the high turnover in staff and particularly emphasises the lack of qualifications which he found in residential workers. This is the case even in the context of numbers of children in public care being greatly reduced over recent years and staff ratios being considerably improved.

12.4 Job satisfaction and job characteristics

We need to have a better understanding of job satisfaction among residential staff and its relationship to stress and turnover. One commentator has made some helpful observations about job satisfaction and its relationship with life-cycle factors in development. He comments:

> "The influence of the life-cycle may explain why so many young people leave the caring professions after only 5 to 10 years service....My argument is that the meaning which therapeutic work has for the intrapsychic balance of a person can contribute to the vulnerability of the professionals, but also the vulnerability of the organization." (Van Eck, 1990)

It is exactly this possible vulnerability of the organization that interests me in so far as it is connected with the way that provision is made for staff needs.

My own research (Challender, 1986) in the area of job characteristics and job satisfaction was an attempt to apply the Job Characteristics model (Hackman & Oldham, 1980) to a residential child care agency. In many ways this study posed more questions than it was able to answer and highlighted the difficulties in assessing job satisfaction in residential staff. Van Eck (op.cit., 1990) makes this point quite strongly:

> "Job satisfaction is a difficult problem in therapeutic communities....we depend on internal criteria since even the external production criterium does not supply us with information on the quality of what we do. Psychiatry, psychotherapy, sociotherapy etc. are 'impossible professions' as Janet Malcolm called psychoanalysis: the objectives are vague, satisfaction is difficult to attain and, when ultimately achieved, it is always late, comes after a long period of effort, and in small dosages."

What is perhaps more accessible to scrutiny is the way in which the job characteristics are designed in care agencies and this is an area where management can use enlightened approaches to benefit both staff and residents.

12.5 Job stress and burnout

Staff frequently complain of organizational factors as contributing to job stress. Studies (e.g. Ledger, 1980) have identified variables contributing to staff dissatisfaction such as long hours, lack of privacy, the demands of difficult clients, financial inequality and severe lack of training opportunities. No doubt we should add the negative image of care work that is currently broadcast by the media. This contributes to a sense of isolation and lack of professional identity. It is interesting to note that Berry's study (1976) pointed to lack of professional support rather than lack of formal training as the major factor affecting provision of 'good enough' care. It is within the grasp of residential managers to attend to some of these factors, but, of course, this does not change the fundamentally stressful nature of the work and the need for help in the area of stress management for individual workers (see Gibson, et al., 1989).

This brings me to the question of the so-called 'burn-out' syndrome. It is certainly referred to by many respected writers in the field (e.g. Cherniss, 1980) as a serious problem which arises in the context of the interpersonal relationship between residential workers and their clients. There is what one might call normal stress in relation to this situation and which can be understood in psychodynamic terms as involving transference and countertransference phenomena. Over and above this there may develop an extreme situation, or burn-out, where a worker collapses under a feeling of contributing much more than is coming back from their clients, supervisors and colleagues. In my experience of the independent sector this syndrome is relatively rare but certainly observable. The low rate may, of course, be related to higher levels of support in private settings and to selectivity over clients. There is likely to be a higher rate in public care and may correspond with high turn-over rates (Cherniss, 1980)

12.6 Coping mechanisms

The study of burn-out does produce insights into coping mechanisms employed by staff in this stressful occupation. For example, there may be present so-called 'detached concern' for clients, intellectualization of situations, compartmentalization of work and professional life, physical withdrawal from clients and reliance upon colleagues for advice, comfort and release of tension. Menzies (1970) was one of the first to study how staff cope with work-related anxiety. She demonstrated how the 'social defence system' of an establishment can be defined by reference to the manner in which staff handle stress. They may do this by splitting off from their clients - a process which may lead to depersonalization, categorization, and denial of the significance of the individual. Staff may also become emotionally detached from the work content through a process of denying their feelings. Task performance is likely to become ritualised with a consequent reduction in risk and the need for decision-making.

Such coping mechanisms, which are akin to burn-out, operate in highly stressful circumstances and will gather momentum if not monitored within the agency and attended to. Elsewhere Menzies (1985) has given a very clear view of how crucial it is for the child care institution and, therefore, it's staff to be functioning at a level which will promote the development of self in the child residents.

12.7 Intrapsychic factors

Clearly residential work requires much personal dedication and commitment, and, furthermore, an ability to retain some level of appropriate detachment to avoid the possibility of getting submerged. Not all workers will have healthy motivations. There are likely to be unhealthy, defensive motivations alongside what-ever altruistic or healthy dedication exists. The very process of being involved in intensive residential therapeutic work often has a defensive function for the worker in his/her attempt to maintain intrapsychic balance. This necessitates continued involvement to maintain the balance and so there develops a clinging to work as part of a coping mechanism which is ultimately self-defeating and may lead to burn-out or at least inefficient task performance. It may also contribute to what has been called the 'shared fantasy' (Van Eck, op cit., 1990) of a group of workers, and this fantasy if not challenged by reality constraints (as might happen in a therapeutic community, for example) will endure in a way which renders the institution vulnerable.

12.8 Support issues

This process of 'shared fantasy' gives a clue to the potential desert island existence of some residential establishments and contains a clear image of isolated groups of staff holding on to each other for support. It emphasises for me the crucial role of external consultants in such establishments and the necessity for effective supervision provided by well-functioning management. When the workforce consists of mainly young people, many of them barely emerged from adolescence and many of them with defensive motivations and needing all-absorbing occupation to maintain intrapsychic balance, it is likely that dependency needs will be acted out in a way that is not in the interests of the residents. Indeed, unwittingly staff may be deriving support from their clients and may relate to the institution as a parent, albeit with strongly ambivalent attitudes to that parent. In this respect a community which relies on such a staff group runs the risk of providing a late adolescent moratorium for young staff who both need and reject some further dependence on parental figures. Such a scenario creates a context for an unhealthy expression of support needs and may be marked by a staff culture permeated with drinking, smoking and dependent behaviour.

12.9 Provision for staff needs

In view of these possibilities how are residential establishments to function effectively in the interests of their clients? How can staff needs, staff organization be provided for to ensure effective primary task performance which will meet the needs of the residents? Hood (1985) proposes a helpful model which takes these factors into account. Such a model distinguishes between those demands which are inevitable and inherent in the residential task and those variables which management can hope to influence and which will affect levels of stress and ability to withstand demands. There are implications in this model for the effective management of many areas of a residential establishment along the lines referred to earlier by Menzies (1985). It is not possible in this contribution to pursue all of these. The area in focus here is provision of support for staff and this will include:

1. Support Objectives
   - Facilitating understanding of the residential task;
   - Maintaining focus on the task;
   - Mitigating stress;
   - Finding solutions to problems encountered in daily living;
   - Assisting professional development.
2. Support Provision
   - Effective management;
   - Good supervision;
   - Administrative support;
   - Appropriate training opportunities;
   - Consultant support;
   - Membership of professional groups and associations.

Supervision is particularly important and is an essential component of an effective support service for residential staff. It provides an assessment of work including, most importantly, recognition of strengths, identification of weaknesses with help to improve them, and a supportive forum for expressing and dealing with the intense feelings which arise in residential group care (Mattingly, 1981; Mutzeck, 1991).

12.10 Conclusion

In this contribution I have mentioned some aspects of residential child care in England today. Numbers of children in care are fewer and changes in policy and legislation are likely to lead to a reduction in the number of residential establishments with an expectation of higher standards of practice. If residential care is to be innovative and offering a high standard of service it will depend on staff who can endure the stress of a very demanding occupation. Some aspects of this stress have been considered along with ideas about how staff employ coping mechanisms to enable them to survive. It is vitally important that managers of residential agencies understand these factors and develop support structures accordingly. Effective supervision is central to such support and will be further enhanced by appropriate use of external consultancy. The latter is especially helpful for residential establishments and communities in view of their natural tendency to develop shared fantasies and to be overwhelmed both by their task and by the group dynamics which inevitably develop.

References

Berry, J. (1975). *Daily experience in residential life.* London: Routledge and Kegan Paul.

Challender, D. (1986). *Job characteristics, job satisfaction and job performance: an investigation of residential workers in a care agency.* Unpublished MSc. Thesis, University of Surrey.

Cherniss, C. (1980). *Staff burnout.* London: Sage.

Gibson, F., McGrath, A., & Reid, N. (1989). Occupational Stress in Social Work. *British Journal of Social Work, 19,* 1-16.

Hackman, J.R. & Oldham, G.R. (1980). *Work redesign.* Reading: Addison-Wesley.

Hood, S. (1985). Staff needs, staff organization and effective primary performance in the residential setting. *International Journal of Therapeutic Communities, 6,* 1, 15-36.

Ledger, R. (1980). Residential Turnover. *Social Work Today, 2,* 14-16.

Mattingly, M. (1981). Occupational stress for group care personnel. In F. Ainsworth & L.C. Fulcher (Eds.), *Group care for children.* New York: Tavistock.

Menzies, I.E.P. (1970). *The functioning of social systems as a defence against anxiety.* London: Tavistock Institute of Human Relations.

Menzies Lyth, I.E.P. (1985). The development of self in children in institutions. *Journal of Child Psychotherapy, 11,* 2, 49-64.

Mutzeck, W. (1991). *Group consultation. Personnel supervision in residential care* (pp. 183-193). Leuven/Amersfoort: Acco.

Utting, W. (1991). *Children in the public care.* London: HMSO.

Van Eck, L. (1990). Leadership and management in psychiatric organizations. *International Journal of Therapeutic Communities, 11,* 149-156.

13 The Large Group: The Heart of The System in Residential Care

A. Ward

13.1 Introduction

This paper explores anxieties amongst residential workers about the use of the large group as a forum for discussion and therapy. It is argued that these fears, although common, are self-perpetuating and anti-task, representing an attempt to deny the reality of living together in groups. By contrast, working with the large group in the form of a daily community meeting of all staff and residents, although difficult to establish and demanding to sustain, can become the central reference-point of daily living and indeed of all therapeutic work in group care settings - 'the heart of the system'.

The aims of this contribution are firstly to identify the nature of the difficulty, secondly to analyze the practical and therapeutic functions of the community meeting in residential settings, and thirdly to discuss the implications of these findings for the training of residential care workers. My overall aim is to argue for establishing a more optimistic and positive self-fulfilling prophecy, so that workers can create opportunities for the creative and beneficial use of large groups - and in particular, so that the practice of the community meeting can become more widely-established in group care.

13.2 The large group and its attendant anxieties

The central fact about residential care is that it involves groups of people - staff and residents - living and working together. They all belong to one large group, whether or not that group becomes formalised into an identified meeting, and whether or not they identify strongly with that group. They all affect each other for better or worse, and while some of these effects are very obvious for all to see, others are much more difficult to detect, although potentially just as powerful.

I should like to call this fact 'undeniable', but my experience tells me that in many places this basic fact is denied, in that residential workers do not engage (or are not encouraged to engage) sufficiently or appropriately in working with the large group. The consequence of this denial is that much of the potential benefit of the residential situation risks being lost or wasted. There may be many reasons for such denial and avoidance, but I would suggest that one important reason is a widespread anxiety among staff (but often also projected onto residents) about being in and working in large groups.

Why are people so anxious about working with large groups? In some ways this is an especially surprising phenomenon in group care, where one might expect the workers to be confident and positive about groupwork, but many residential workers do seem to lack the confidence to work with the whole group of staff and users, and this anxiety is sometimes so great that it seems to lead into a self-fulfilling prophecy, whereby workers anticipate difficulty with large groups, and their anxiety brings that very difficulty into the group.

In the literature on groupwork in group care, many authors reveal considerable unease with using the large group. For example, an otherwise-constructive paper by Allan Brown (1990) which provides a useful framework for analysing 'The Group Mosaic in Residential and Day Centre Settings', nevertheless offers a bleak view of working with large groups. Brown describes community meetings thus:

"They are sometimes fairly disastrous, and can be destructive, the reason for this being that large groups (say of more than 20 persons) can be very frightening places" (Brown, 1990, 277)

This statement is unfortunate in that it risks perpetuating the myth of the destructive large group. My own view is that not everyone does find large groups so frightening and destructive. The reality, surely, is that while it may be true that some people, both staff and users, do find the thought of being in a large group frightening, it is also true that many people find membership of any size of group

threatening. Nitsun (1991), for example, argues that there are strong 'anti-group' feelings in many people (both professionals and others), and suggests that people may feel uncomfortable with the very idea of joining a group for a variety of reasons -
"I believe that there is a widespread and fundamental resistance to groups, arising partly from the wish for the fantasied, idealized containment of the two-person relationship and the threat that the group poses to this fantasy" (Nitsun, 1991).
Although Nitsun is writing about the small group in particular, there are clear parallels with commonly-expressed feelings about the large group.

On the other hand, perhaps the fear of the large group in particular relates to (among other things) an intuitive grasp of the power of the phenomenon. The large group is a powerful experience, although this power can be harnessed to beneficial ends, and a successful and well-run large group can be a liberating and empowering experience. It may be that many group-workers and residential workers have not experienced being a member of a successful large group themselves (in fact they may have experienced quite the opposite) and thus they do not carry within them a belief that such a thing is possible.
Here the importance of training is obvious, in that it is essential that training for groupwork (and residential work) should do more than merely confirm people in their original prejudices and anxieties, and should require them to experience, think and learn about the many and various contexts of groupwork, and should give them access to positive models of many different types of group, rather than only the traditional 'small group'. This is not to deny, of course, that people will then develop a preference for working with a certain size and type of group, just as they will opt for a certain style of group leadership, but these choices should be as explicit and understood as possible.
I should acknowledge that there is some debate about precisely when a 'small' group becomes 'large' - for example, Hopper and Weyman (1975) point out that for some people a small group consists of no more than 5 - 7 members, whereas for others a group does not become large until there are more than 16 members. For some people a large group seems to mean 'a group just larger than I can

cope with', whereas for others a small group is probably 'a group which is so small that I feel claustrophobic'.

Perhaps a more useful approach to this issue would be to think in terms of the *proportions and context* of the group rather than its size. Thus a group of 14 people which meets as part of a conference for 200 people will probably be experienced by many members as a small group, whereas a group of 14 people who comprise the total group of staff and residents of an adolescent psychiatric unit is probably experienced by most members as large. Somewhere in the middle comes the concept of the Median Group, a term sometimes used to refer to groups of 16 - 30 people, although here again the boundaries between one size of group and another will blur according to the subjective experience of the participants. (See Kreeger (1975) for further discussion of large group phenomena.)

13.3 The community meeting

In the particular context of a residential setting, the 'large group' usually means the total group of staff and residents, and a principal forum for the meeting-together of this large group will be what is usually known as the House Meeting or Community Meeting. The literature on such meetings relates mostly to the therapeutic community, and especially the therapeutic community for adults with mental health problems (see, for example, IJTC 1987). However, the community meeting need not be restricted to such settings; indeed, a case can be mounted for the use of community meetings in many other group care settings - Family Centres, probation work (see Cook, 1988), and residential settings for various groups (e.g. with young adolescents, Worthington, 1990). I have described elsewhere (Ward, 1984), the introduction of community meetings in residential work with young children.

Since many residential units for children and young people are now very small units, even 'family-sized', it is important to be clear that working with the 'large group' applies even in these settings. For the purposes of this paper, the 'large group' refers to the total living-group of a residential setting, whether that is a group of 8 or a group of 48. What is important is that the total living-group of residents and staff should meet together on a planned and regular basis, in recognition of the fact that they live and work together.

Now, bearing in mind the discomforts, fears and resistances mentioned above in relation to large groups, it is evident at once that for such a meeting to be successful, certain conditions must be established. In particular, all of the participants will need to be clear and in broad agreement about the specific functions and possibilities of the meeting - otherwise (as with any other method of work) people will be left uncertain and may become anxious, filling in the absence of declared and agreed functions with assumed functions of their own invention, such as the persecution of the powerless. It is important, therefore, to be clear about the range of possible functions of the community meeting.

13.3.1 The functions of the community meeting

Among the various functions of the community meeting, I propose below a number which seem important in creating an argument for the greater use of this method. This first list covers the practical and social-emotional functions of the community meeting, and it will be evident to the reader that, if the meeting does fulfil these functions, it will become a central focus of all the work of the community - the place to which and from which all important business is taken.

1. Planning the events of the day/week together, so that everyone knows what is happening and why;
2. Reviewing what has happened during the past day/week and why: learning from experience;
3. Discussing the rules of the house: whose rules they are, how they are enforced and why;
4. Discussing the routines of the house: residents and workers evaluate and change their daily living experience;
5. Problem-solving: for users to bring conflicts, unsolved losses, confusions, etc. for resolution within the security of the group;
6. Handling general feedback between users and staff on behaviour and its effects, etc;
7. Working on understanding, predicting and dealing with the feelings involved in living together in a group, e.g. the comings and goings of users and staff; inconsistencies thrown up by

shift-work; plus feelings related to issues of power, prejudice and dependency;

8. Handling crises, e.g. emergency admissions, major disturbances, etc;

9. 'Assembly': getting everyone together, acknowledging the fact of living together and having to get on with one another;

10. Working with the 'whole person', encouraging people to give as well as take, enableas well as disrupt, etc, and enabling all members to perceive each other as whole people as well as having roles e.g. staff, user.

In addition, however, there are other functions which the community meeting can play in the life of a residential unit, and especially in a unit which has therapeutic aims. Some of these other functions are suggested by Melvyn Rose thus:

'The subject matter of community meetings always was complex. Trying to make sense of relationships, trying to describe feelings, and trying to describe their origins required the youngsters to develop new ways of thinking as well as speaking' (Rose, 1990, 130).

The community meeting offers the children the opportunity for developing such new ways of thinking by performing a number of therapeutic functions, for example:

1. Providing a central focus and reference point for 'The work of the day' (Kennedy, 1989), i.e. enabling maximum learning to be derived from the handling of significant issues arising in the everyday life of the group.

2. Offering a collective sense of 'containment' for troubled individuals and groups, in the sense in which this term is used by Bion (1962) and others: the bearing of anxiety, and the ability to think about and recognize mental pain.

3. Providing a place for the large group to struggle with achieving its potential for mutual help and healing, and with comprehending its own group-identity or 'group ego' (Worthington, 1990, 101).

4. Providing a place in which unconscious phenomena such as the 'reflection process' may be understood and resolved, as a means towards achieving the sense of containment and thus the healing potential described above (see 13.3.2).

5.   Providing a forum in which issues of personal and social power within the group may be safely raised and learned-from.

Some may argue that it is artificial to separate the practical from the therapeutic functions of the community meeting in this way. In some communities, on the other hand, clear distinctions are drawn between therapy-meetings and business-meetings, while some communities evolve different functions for e.g. 'Morning Meetings' and 'Evening Meetings'. My own view is that, however these patterns and distinctions develop during the evolution of any given community, unless the practical functions are being achieved, there is no chance of achieving the therapeutic functions. In other words, the meeting has to succeed at an immediate and practical level for everyone to feel it is worth investing in. In some places, indeed, the practical functions will suffice. Where people have been unsuccessful in attempting to implement a system of community meetings, I would suspect that they were trying to be 'therapeutic' before they were being genuinely useful: this is how group-members become alienated, frightened and angry. Eric Butlin says: 'An institution can be run at a management level without therapy, but therapy cannot exist without management' (Butlin, 1975). Fear of the large group seems to me very close to the fear evoked by the fantasy of therapy without management - a fear of being swallowed up by the ocean, of being overpowered.

13.3.2 A note on the reflection process

The concept of the 'reflection process' refers to the phenomenon whereby the behaviour or emotions of one individual or group may unconsciously reflect or 'mirror' those of another (see Mattinson, 1970). Thus the dynamics of interresident relationships or of resident-to-staff interactions may be recreated within the staff team (and vice versa). For example, in one unit for adolescents, a sudden increase in sexual acting-out among the residents caused confusion and concern among the staff team, until discussion between the staff team and their consultant revealed that a secret sexual relationship which had developed recently between two key staff-members had been causing confusion and jealousy within the team (much of it unconscious), and that the young people had been excited and provoked by this atmosphere. Once this connection was established and understood within the team, the atmosphere in the unit began to return to normal. Similarly, current events or moods in external social or political groupings may have considerable impact upon the internal social climate of the residential unit. This phenomenon is familiar in general terms to many residential workers, and in its various manifestations it often helps to explain events and moods in a residential group which are otherwise difficult to understand, yet it is often difficult to detect in practice, and even more problematic to explain and to learn from. The community meeting, by making such phenomena available for public scrutiny in the large group, may help to make these phenomena manifest, understood, and thus available to be harnessed for their therapeutic potential. The fear and anxiety which is generated by the absence of understanding can thus be allayed, and the community meeting can play a significant role in creating the required understanding.

13.4 Training

Finally, I wish to return to training. If residential workers are going to be more confident, knowledgeable and skilled in leading and understanding the large group, they will have to learn by experience. Training courses will therefore need to include practical as well as theoretical work on large group phenomena. In particular, I want to point out the relevance for training of the phenomenon of the Reflection Process as described above.

The concept of the Reflection Process suggests that the various patterns of interaction between staff, residents and others will also be re-created in training - and indeed that this is a necessary phenomenon through which issues arising in the work can be 'processed' into useful learning. In order to facilitate this process, the curriculum design of training courses must incorporate a range of working methods which will adequately reflect the modes of practice in the settings from which course-members are drawn (I am following here the principle that the mode of training should match the mode of practice [Ward, 1990]). In the case of residential care, training methods will therefore include elements of individual work and consultation, small group work, informal 'working alongside', and in particular, large group work.

The postgraduate Diploma/MA in Therapeutic Child Care at the University of Reading has been designed to operationalize this principle. In particular, each day in college for the students starts and finishes with a joint Meeting of staff and students. These meetings serve several purposes, each of which has some parallels with the use of meetings in the therapeutic community. The Opening Meeting is intended to enable students to 'tune in' again to working in college and with the other group members, to share information and feelings about their last week's work, and to anticipate the process and content of the day's work. The Closing Meeting is intended to bring the day's work together and finish it appropriately, and to encourage analysis of and reflection upon the whole day's work.

These meetings are used for discussing feelings as well as facts, and just like a community meeting, they need to be firmly managed in respect of time-boundaries and other boundaries. In terms of the Reflection Process, the process of these meetings is probably influenced at least as much by the members' unconscious reflection of what is happening to them in their place of work as they are by their conscious analysis of the information which they bring. My hypothesis is that this process of reflection, and the learning which grows from it, is facilitated by the fact that the style and structure of these meetings bears considerable similarity to the way in which the community meeting operates in the therapeutic communities.

There is also an Experiential Group (led by a group analyst) which runs throughout this Course, and which has direct parallels with the staff sensitivity and consultation groups in many therapeutic communities. The aim of this group is to enable students to reflect upon their personal experience in relation to their work, their training and each other, and to enable them to deal with individual and inter-personal problems arising within the group and to learn from these.

This group thus not only enables students to work on 'here and now' issues related to the group and to individual personal concerns, but it also allows for further reflection on issues related to working in the large group both in the communities themselves and on the course.

Thus students gain the experience of being in and working in a large group, and have further opportunities to reflect on this experience in other groups, as well as learning about the theory of large-group work through seminars etc. The aim of this approach to training is to encourage students to feel more skilled and confident in working with the large group, and thereby to spread the message that the power of the large group can be harnessed as both a practical and a therapeutic tool.

13.5 Conclusion

I began this paper with the question, 'Why are people so anxious about working with large groups?', and in the course of this contribution I have suggested several answers, most of them relating to fear of the unknown:
1. Fear based upon a resistance to groups in general;
2. Fear related to an intuitive but misinterpreted grasp of the power of the large group;
3. Fear and anxiety generated by not understanding unconscious phenomena such as the Reflection process;
4. Anxiety raised by confusion and uncertainty about the specific functions and possibilities of the large group.
5. Fear evoked by the fantasy of therapy without management.

Since there is so much fear of that which is not known or not understood, I am proposing that the answer lies principally in training, and particularly in creating the opportunities on training courses for people to gain positive experience of being in, and working in, large groups.

References

Bion, W.R. (1962). *Learning from experience*. London: Heinemann.
Brown, A. (1990). Groupwork with a difference: the group 'mosaic' in residential and day care settings. *Groupwork*, 3, 269-285.
Cook, R. (1988). A non-residential therapeutic community used as an alternative to custody. *International Journal of Therapeutic Communities*, 9, 55-64.

Butlin, E. (1975). Institutionalization, management structure and therapy in residential work with emotionally disturbed children. *British Journal of Social Work, 5,* 283-295.

Hopper, E. & Weyman, A. (1975). A sociological view of large groups. In L. Kreeger [ed.], *The large group. Dynamics and therapy* (pp. 159-189). London: Karnac.

International Journal of Therapeutic Communities, 8 (1987). Special Issue: The Patient-Staff community meeting (ed.: L. Greene). No 2.

Kennedy, R. (1987). The work of the day. In R. Kennedy, A. Heymans & L. Tischler [eds.], *The family as in-patient.* Families and adolescents at the Cassell Hospital. Free Association Books.

Kreeger, L. (Ed.) (1975). *The large group. Dynamics and therapy.* London: Karnac.

Mattinson, J. (1975). *The reflection process in casework supervision.* London: Institute of Marital Studies.

Nitsun, M. (1991). The anti-group: destructive forces in the group and their therapeutic potential. *Group Analysis, 24,* 7-20.

Rose, M. (1990). *Healing hurt minds.* London: Routledge.

Ward, A. (1984). All you can do is bring your own self. *Community Care, 17.*

Ward, A. (1990). *The Reflection Process in the supervision and training of group care workers.* Unpublished paper given at International Special Education Congress, University of Wales, Cardiff.

Worthington, A. (1990). The function of the community meeting in a therapeutic community for pre- and young adolescents. *International Journal of Therapeutic Communities, 11,* 95-102.

14 The Enhancement of Professionality of Residential Child Care Workers

F.M. Edens

14.1 Introduction

Since 1974, the section of Individually Applied Psychology of the department of Personality and Educational Psychology from the University of Groningen has been concerned with the development, implementation, and evaluation of structured training methods and training programmes in professional social skills. The main objective for those who follow these training programmes is to become skilled at conducting professional conversations like, for instance, the interview.

This contribution concerns the history of the project 'The Enhancement of Professionality of Residential Child Care Workers', the development of a training programme for care workers, and the evaluation of this programme.

14.2 The history of the project

For several years now, the section of Individually Applied Psychology has worked together with the field of residential child care. This led to the development of a social skills programme for mentally retarded youngsters (Van der Zee, Van der Molen & Van der Beek, 1989). Care workers were trained to execute this social skills programme with their own group of youngsters. The programme was called the 'Goldstein training' after Arnold P. Goldstein, who pointed out the need for a structured learning programme for clients from lower socio-economic backgrounds (Goldstein, 1973).

The Goldstein training was a success (Bleeker, 1990), and child care institutions asked if it would be possible to develop a new programme. This new programme should focus on the care workers themselves in stead of on the youngsters, and deal with the enhancement of professionality of child care workers. Furthermore, contacts with schools that prepare their students for child care work led to the conclusion that a need was felt for a training in which theoretical knowledge would be put into practice. Finally, Dutch literature (Van Hekken, De Ruyter & Sanders Woudstra, 1987) also mentioned a lack of practical methodology. Therefore, the care workers project was started with the objective to develop, implement, and evaluate a training programme for residential child care workers. The programme should result in care workers dealing more effectively with difficult individual or group situations involving youngsters. The project is carried out in order of the N.I.Z.W., the Netherlands Institute of Care and Welfare. The N.I.Z.W. is the national institute responsible for research and development in the field of care and welfare.

14.3 The development of the training programme

14.3.1 Objectives
The program that was developed was called 'Skills for Residential Child Care Workers'. The three main objectives of the training were:
- to increase knowledge on how to apply skills for dealing with difficult situations.
- to extend the behaviour repertoire of skills for actually dealing with those difficult situations.
- to teach an attitude based on the principles of 'directivity', acceptance and reinforcement. Directivity means to be able to work according to plan. In a more general way, one could say that a directive care worker is someone who runs a tight ship. Acceptance means to be able to show that you understand a youngsters feelings and that you accept him or her as a person. Reinforce-

ment means to be able to focus on the things these youngsters do well, in stead of the things they do wrong.

These three principles have been adopted from the Goldstein workshop, in which care workers were trained to execute the Goldstein training.

14.3.2 The content of the training programme

The content of the training came about partly on the basis of literature research, partly by interviewing 20 residential child care workers about the difficulties which they encounter in handling youngsters. This resulted in a training programme that consisted of three modules: basic skills, individual contacts with youngsters and their parents, and difficult group situations. These modules contain the following elements:

I   Basic skills.

This section is concerned with: attending behaviour, asking questions, paraphrasing of content and summarizing, reflection of feeling, and structuralizing a mentor conversation.

II   Individual contacts with youngsters and their parents.

In this section central topics are: situation clarification, teaching of skills to youngsters, receiving criticism, giving criticism, and bringing bad news. Situation clarification means being able to recognize and discuss ambiguities or misunderstandings occurring during the ongoing dialogue.

III   Difficult group situations.

The third module is about: directing a group discussion, conflict management (how to intervene in and solve a quarrel between youngsters), dealing with provocations and handling outsiders in the group. Outsiders can be broadly classified into two groups: very shy, non-assertive children or very aggressive, dominating children.

Each module consisted of 5 half-day sessions.

14.3.3 The educational method

The educational method used to reach the above mentioned three objectives was based on Ivey's 'microtraining' method (Ivey & Authier, 1978). This is a highly structured training method in which skills are taught by using the following elements:

- theoretical instruction

- modelling (the demonstration of a right and wrong example of the skill by a video model)
- practise by means of role play
- feedback
- transfer to work situation by means of homework.

The use of video modelling meant that three videotapes had to be made, the content of which corresponded with the content of the three modules. Before the start of a training session, trainees were supposed to do some homework, which consisted of reading some paragraphs as well as a practical assignment. The training itself started with a discussion of the theory. Next, the video tape was played. Each skill or situation was displayed by means of a wrong and a right example in which the skills were ineffectively or effectively used. An example usually takes about 2 to 5 minutes. Trainees were asked to observe the behaviour of the model on aspects which were discussed in the theory. After an example had been played, trainees were asked to state their observations. Sometimes a group exercise in practising the skill followed. Finally, the group split up into smaller groups for practising by means of role play. A session ended, of course, with homework.

14.4 The evaluation method

As was mentioned earlier on, the training had three objectives:
- to increase knowledge on how to apply skills for dealing with difficult situations.
- extend the behaviour repertoire of skills for actually dealing with these situations.
- to teach an attitude based on the principles of directivity, acceptance and reinforcement.

In order to investigate if these objectives were attained, several evaluation instruments were developed. A behavioral test was constructed to evaluate improvement in skills for handling difficult group situations, a knowledge test to evaluate improvement in knowledge, as well as a learner report in which trainees could report on what they themselves considered the most important things they had learned, and a course evaluation questionnaire for evaluating the training programme. Because the material from the learner report has not been interpreted yet, this report will not be discussed.

14.4.1 *The evaluation instruments*

The behavioral test consisted of a simulation and an assessment list. In the simulation subjects were required to direct a group meeting with four actors who played the part of slow-learning adolescents. These actors were trained to react in a standardized way to the actions of the subjects. All simulations were recorded on video. Later on, observers scored the behaviour of the subjects on the assessment list. On the assessment list, six abilities that were considered essential in handling difficult group situations were translated into behavioral categories. All categories were scored on a five point scale. The abilities were described as:
- regulating ability, i.e. the ability to structure the situation and to keep an overview,
- empathic ability, i.e. the ability to understand youngsters' feelings and treat them with respect.
- stimulating ability, i.e. the ability to encourage others to state their view, or to encourage behaviour.
- the ability to handle conflicts
- problem solving ability,
- assertiveness

Together, these abilities were assumed to cover the complex ability of handling difficult group situations. Two parallel versions of the test were developed.

The knowledge test was a paper-and-pencil test, designed to measure knowledge about the content of the training curriculum. Two parallel versions were developed. In both the case of the behavioral test and the knowledge test, the two test versions were distributed evenly over treatment and control group, as well as over care workers and students.

In the course evaluation questionnaire, questions were asked about the organization of the training, the educational method, the content of the training programme, and the amount of time that was spent on each subject of the programme. All answers were scored on a five point scale.

14.4.2 *The design*

Two groups of subjects participated in the investigation, a treatment group, consisting of 29 persons, and a control group, consisting of 26 persons. All subjects were either care workers or students from a school that prepares for child care work.

In January the treatment group took both tests, the behavioral test as well as the knowledge test. Next, this group participated in the training and afterwards, in April, took two parallel versions of both tests. Half a year later, they came back for a follow-up measurement, in which the procedure repeated itself. The control group received no training at first but took the tests at the same time as the treatment group. This group is being trained at the moment and will also take part in a posttraining as well as a follow-up measurement. This design, a so called pretest-posttest-follow up-control group design without random assignment (Cook & Campbell, 1979), is used to make sure that any improvement after the training can be attributed to the training and not to some other cause. A follow-up measurement was included to investigate if posttraining results were maintained over a half-year period. The results that will be discussed in the next paragraph concern the period from January to April, 1991.

14.5 Results

14.5.1 *The reliability of the tests*

To start with the behavioral test, the internal consistency of the assessment list, estimated by coefficient alpha, was substantial, .83. This high level of reliability is striking, in view of the small number of scales on which the assessment list has been based.

In order to estimate the interrater reliability, Pearson product moment correlations between raters were computed. Correlations were based on the total scores (i.e. the sum of the scores on the six scales). The correlations were substantial, varying from .76 for raters 1 and 3 and .81 for raters 1 and 2, to .83 for raters 2 and 3. These results indicate that the raters agreed closely on their ratings of the behavioral assessment list.

The knowledge test contained 11 open-ended questions and five multiple choice questions. With the open ended questions three sorts of scores were possible: wrong, right and half-right. Because the

answers were easy to score, two raters rated half of all the tests each. The internal consistency of the two versions was .63 for version A en .66 for version B (posttest measurement).
In short, the reliability of the tests was high on the behavioral test and moderate on the knowledge test.

14.5.2 The course evaluation questionnaire
This questionnaire contained over 50 questions on aspects of the training. Some points of interest to a wider audience have been selected; questions which concerned the organizational details of the training were left out.

Table 1   Course Evaluation Means

	M	sd	Scale description
Method	4.27	.29	1 negative 3 neutral 5 positive
Usefulness skills	4.14	.36	
Amount of time spent on skills	3.16	.19	1 too much 3 enough 5 not enough

Trainees were asked to rate each part of the educational method, the usefulness of each skill, and the amount of time spent on that skill. The results of these questions were summarized. Table 1 shows that the trainees were satisfied about the training programme.

Table 2   Means on Behavioral test and Knowledge test

	PRE TRAINING				POST TRAINING			
	CONTROL		TREATMENT		CONTROL		TREATM.	
	M	sd	M	sd	M	sd	M	sd
Beh.	2.85	.56	2.69	.44	2.69	.54	3.25	.42
Know.	26.2	4.64	27.8	4.27	27.7	4.74	31.5	4.12

Beh. = behavioral test, know. = knowledge test.

The scores on the six abilities of the behavioral test were compressed to one mean score (table 2). Before the training, the treatment group

184

and the control group did not differ significantly from each other on the pretest measurement. Posttraining means are as follows: the control group scored 2.69 on the behavioral test whereas the treatment group scored 3.25. With the knowledge test, the results were 27.7 for the control group and 31.5 for the treatment group (the score range on the knowledge test varies from 15 to 45). So the treatment group scores higher on both tests, compared with the control group. A multivariate analysis of variance was used to investigate if these differences between groups were significant (table 3).

Table 3   *MANOVA results for behavioral test and knowledge test*

Multivariate			Univariate			
F	Df	Sig		F	Df	Sig
12.01	2.00	.000	Knowledge	4.66	1.53	.035
			Behaviour	23.98		.000

Table 3 shows a main effect for group and time of measurement. This means that after having received the training, the treatment group scored significantly higher than the control group on both tests. Both tests contributed to that result, especially the behavioral test.

A MANOVA on the six abilities of the behavioral test was done to see whether the treatment group made progress with all abilities, or just with some.

Table 4   *MANOVA results for the scales of the behaviourial test*

Multivariate			Univariate			
F	Df	Sig		F	DF	Sig
3.73	6.00	.004	regulating a.	15.75	1.53	.001
			empathic a.	17.09		.001
			stimulating a.	17.84		.001
			conflict m.	5.96		.018
			problem sol.a.	9.25		.004
			assertiveness	6.86		.011

The treatment group scored significantly higher on all scales. The first three scales, regulating ability, empatic ability, and stimulating ability contributed especially to this result. A possible explanation is that these three scales resemble the three attitude aspects of directivity, acceptance, and reinforcement. During the training, a lot of time was spent on these aspects. To summarize, the test results are positive: the treatment group improves significantly in knowledge and behaviour, compared to the control group.

14.6 Discussion

Two conclusions can be drawn. First of all, in view of the parallelity and reliability of the two versions of the test, both have proven to be useful instruments for evaluation research. The tests might be put to a wider use by employing them for selection purposes. Second, the training appears to have a significantly positive effect on the behaviour of child care workers and students. However, this does not automatically imply that a transfer will take place from the training situation to the work situation. Literature on the issue of generalizability (Bellack & Hersen, 1979; Martin, 1990) does not justify such a inference. Assessment of skills by collegues or observations at work are possible methods to investigate to what extent application of skills as a result of training takes place. Of course, the last mentioned research methods are not without disadvantages, such as the difficult standardization of the work situation.

A question that has to be asked is whether third variables might have explained the progress of the experimental group. A check was made for the potential effects of test version and stooge group on the results. They did not have a confounding effect. The research outcome was also independent of the fact whether the subjects were child care workers or students. A further detrimental factor might be that the experimental group had an advantage over the control group on relevant variables that were not controlled for, such as level of education. As control group scores were somewhat higher than experimental group scores at pretest measurement, variables not controlled for were not considered detrimental.

Overall we conclude - with the above-mentioned restrictions - that the training is effective in enhancing child care workers' professional attitude and skills. In the future the training will become available for residential training institutes and in-service training facilities in the Netherlands and Belgium.

References

Bellack, A.S., & Hersen, M. (1979). *Research and practice in social skills training.* New York/London: Plenum Press.

Bleeker, J.K. (1990). *Effecten van een sociaal redzaamheidsprogramma voor zwakbegaafde jongeren.* Ph.D. Dissertation, University of Groningen.

Cook, T.D., & Campbell, D.T. (1979). *Quasi-experimentation, design & analysis issues for field settings.* Boston: Houghton Mifflin Company.

Edens, F.M. (1990). *Vaardigheden voor groepsleiders* (Cursusklapper). Groningen: University of Groningen, Department of Personality and Educational Psychology (unpublished).

Goldstein, A.P. (1973). *Structured learning therapy, toward a psychotherapy for the poor.* New York: Academic Press.

Hekken, S.M.J. van, Ruyter, P.A. de, Sanders-Woudstra, J.A.R. (1987). *Residentiële jeugdhulpverlening, voorwerp van aanhoudende zorg.* Rapport ten behoeve van Ministerie van WVC en Ministerie van Justitie.

Ivey, A.E., & Authier, J. (1978). *Microcounseling. Innovations in interviewing, counseling, psychotherapy and psychoeducation.* Springfield: Charles C. Thomas.

Martin, J. (1990). Confusions in psychological skills training. *Journal of Counseling & Development, 68,* 402-407.

Smit, G.N. (1991). *De evaluatie van de training 'Vaardigheden voor groepsleiders' met behulp van een gedragstest en een vragenlijst. Stageverslag.* Groningen: University of Groningen, Department of Personality and Educational Psychology (unpublished).

Teurlings, L. (1991). *De evaluatie van de training 'Vaardigheden voor groepsleiders' met behulp van een kennistoets. Projectverslag.* Groningen: University of Groningen, Department of Personality and Educational Psychology (unpublished).

Zee, S.A.M. van der, Molen, H.T. van der, & Beek, D.T. van der (1989). *Sociale vaardigheden voor zwakbegaafde jongeren. Praktijkboek Goldsteinttraining.* Deventer: Van Loghum Slaterus.

15 The Climate in a Residential Setting; A Theoretical Framework and its Applications

K. Visser

15.1 Introduction

In this chapter I will give a brief explanation of a model for improving and using the social climate of a residential system. The model is based on my experience as a group worker, staff member and consultant for residential treatment. Olga Houweling-Meyers and I have elaborated the model through study and research, and through discussions and workshops with skilled, experienced workers.

15.2 The social system: the core of residential treatment

A residential institute must be perceived as a social system - a social system in which all actions are aimed at improving the social system and the participation of the clients in the system. Residential treatment is not simply the sum of advice, therapy and care for individual clients taking place, more or less accidentally, in a residential institute.

The importance of considering and developing a residential institute as a social system was emphasized decades ago by several researchers and field workers. Polsky and others have done a lot of research on improving the social system of an institute (Polsky & Claster, 1968). Goffman has shown us the effects a neglected system can have on clients (Goffman, 1961). In this chapter it is impossible to do justice to their contributions. It is, however, necessary to make one remark. Polsky and others elaborated on a model for improving the social system. When we take a closer look at Polsky's research we see a shift in focus from the system to the individual client. His instructions: monitoring, guiding, supporting, integrating - are aimed at the person instead of the system.

We had to come to the conclusion that he does not offer a model for the improvement of the system itself. In spite of this valuable research we still need a model for improving residential institutes as social systems.

15.3 A theory of social systems is indispensable

People create social systems. People are members of social systems. People need social systems. People grow and develop by being members of meaningful social systems.

In this chapter I am not going to argue about these matters. Nor am I going to prove the relevance of these statements. I will, however, stress the conviction that though psychological and educational theories are of great value, they can only be effective when supported by a meaningful social system. That is why we need a theory of social systems. The effects of existing individual treatment theories have diverted our attention away from the social system.

In our search for a theory of social systems we could not use existing theories because ultimately they all aim at improving individual behaviour or communication between individuals. There is no theory that focuses directly on the social system itself. Once we reached this conclusion, we decided to go back to the roots of system theory: General System Theory. Experience and study make it quite clear that general system theory cannot be applied directly to social systems. All its applications cannot do justice to the special features of a social system. The models for application are unable to deal with questions about significance, goal development, energy within the system and the ever-changing structure of the social system. Yet, general system theory offers us valuable insights into social systems. To apply the theory to social systems it must, however, be adapted and transformed into a social system theory. In our elaboration we have concentrated on similarities and differences.

General system theory states that all systems whether they are physical, biological or social depend on the same characteristics for their existence and development. Every system has a structure, more or less open boundaries, depends upon the energy of the parts which hold the system together and keep the system in motion, and finally, every system is goal-oriented. Structure, boundaries, energy and goals must be tuned in a way that enables the system to match the goals and ambitions of the parts of the system itself, and to correspond with the surroundings. The characteristic differences between social systems and other systems occur because social systems are created by people. They are created by people and their existence depends on people. The characteristics of social systems are not predetermined but determined and re-determined by the people within the system.

We have already stated that everyone needs social systems, that is why we create social systems. Whether we will be a member of social systems or not is not a matter of free choice. People are, however, reasonably free to choose their own systems and people are capable of affecting their systems. Everyone has the capacity to know whether a system or his membership in a system is beneficial to himself and others. We feel and know whether a system is beneficial to us and we can act according to that knowledge. That puts a strain on residential treatment. Care and therapy cannot compensate for the fact that in most cases the social system is not chosen by the client. The success or failure of treatment is determined by the amount of meaning the client awards to the system. Consequently we need a model for the development of significance of social systems, e.g. residential institutes. Unfortunately most models for treatment, care or therapy reduce the client's opportunities for relevant partnership in the residential institute and thereby reduce significance.

Before I move on to the development of the social system I will point out the difference between residential treatment and other kinds of treatment and therapy. Admission to a residential institute means quite plainly: 'You are unable to cope with the everyday social systems everybody can cope with, or you are not allowed to continue coping the way you do'. Out-patients remain inside their social systems during therapy or treatment.

They can use those systems for experiments with new ways of coping. In residential treatment the client is cut off from many of the opportunities that other people have. It is my conviction that the first obligation of residential treatment is to offer new opportunities for experiments in coping. The first obligation is to offer a meaningful social system in which clients can learn how to cope and to participate.

15.4 A meaningful social system

As I mentioned before our criteria for developing social systems are derived from general system theory. We adopt the assumption that social systems show the same inherent features as are found in all other systems. Common sense and experience of over thirty years validate that assumption. If we apply this assumption to residential treatment we can evaluate it by investigating:
- the development of goals;
- the utilization of energy;
- the development of structure;
- the exchange with surroundings.

The ways in which goals, energy, structure and surroundings are dealt with determine the climate and the significance of the institute. Significance from a system perspective means that the members of the institute are able to benefit from the energy everybody brings into the system. The significance and power of the system are determined by the notion that people inside the system need each other for the achievement of their goals.

15.5 Four system characteristics

The following scheme clarifies the four functions which have to be fulfilled within a social system. As social systems are never motionless but always subject to motion and change, fulfilment of the four functions is a never-ending process.

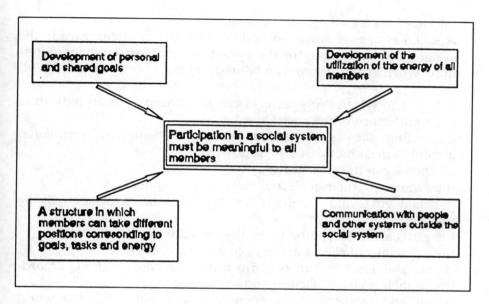

Figure 1   *Four system functions*

The functions are:
- *Goal development*
  The members of social system must be supported to discover, develop and express their personal goals. Stimulation of mutual support in discovering goals emphasizes the significance of being together.
- *Utilization of energy*
  The attainment of goals is dependent upon available energy. The energy of the participants must be evoked and supported. Energy must be directed towards the goals. Experience makes it quite clear that all energy has to be used. When energy is suppressed it will always be used to disturb goals.
- *Development of structure*
  Tasks must be distributed and positions assigned in such a way that capacities of the members are utilized to a maximum to reach the goals.

- *Communication with the surroundings*
  A social system is never isolated. The impact of forces outside the system and the impact of the system on the surroundings determine whether the system can be meaningful.

The degree to which these features can be performed is an indication of the significance of the social system.
Summarizing the functions for residential treatment, residential treatment is meaningful and helpful when:
- all clients can develop goals;
- they can share their goals and support each other;
- personal goals and the goals set for residential treatment can be matched;
- the goals are achieved by using the capacities of the clients;
- the capacities of clients are evoked and encouraged;
- clients and workers can perform tasks and take positions according to their goals, capacities and situations;
- clients and workers are in open communication with the world outside;
- treatment stimulates clients to perform roles outside the institute.

Years of experience tell us that a major violation of these rules is an exclusive dedication to 'care' or 'control'. This dedication will obstruct the energy of clients and as a consequence goals will be disturbed.

15.6 Application of the theory

Developing the social system of treatment means making judgments about the four criteria related to a social system. Based on that judgment, remedial undertaken.
Finally I will explain a model of application in residential treatment.
So far now I have applied the model as a consultant in residential youth treatment, a centre for abused women and children, institutes for mentally retarded people and a detention centre.
To exert influence upon a social system, we need information about the system. When I say *we* need information, I mean all members of the system: workers, children and me, the consultant. By using a

model of action research, gathering information becomes a process of experimentation and empowerment.

Our first step is do a system analysis. The analysis offers us themes to work on. We could make an analysis of the system at any time, with any group, using any case. According to general system theory the state of the system is reflected in every part and every event.

At first I used the theory as a background framework for analyzing critical incidents.

The themes to work on and the critical incidents were introduced by the staff members and group workers in the consult project.

For two years I have worked with questionnaires on the four system features to come to an analysis of the social system. The advantage of working with questionnaires is that background theory becomes explicit to all members in the project and they all can become participants on rather than users of the project.

First I will describe the design of the questionnaires. After that I will give an example of the application.

So far, I have developed three questionnaires reflecting the four system criteria. Consequently they contain questions about goals and the development of goals, questions about energy, meaning capacities and the evocation of capacities of all members of the system, questions about structure and the degree to which members can affect the structure, and questions about communication with the environment of the system.

There is one questionnaire about conditions the system offers to the workers as perceived by the workers; one questionnaire about conditions the system offers to the clients as perceived by the workers, and one questionnaire about conditions the system offers to the clients as perceived by the clients. The three questionnaires run parallel to each other.

For example: questions about goals.

In the questionnaire about conditions the system offers to the workers, as perceived by the workers:

1. Are there goals concerning your professional development that your colleagues or superiors want you to achieve?
2. Do you have your own professional goals you want to achieve?
3. Are the others familiar with the professional goals you want to achieve?

4. Are you supported in reaching your professional goals?

In the questionnaire about conditions the system offers to the clients, as perceived by the workers:
1. Does the client know the goals we have developed for his treatment?
2. Is the client stimulated to develop personal goals?
3. Is the client stimulated to share his personal goals with the others?
4. Is the client supported in reaching his personal goals?

In the questionnaire about conditions the system offers to the clients, as perceived by the clients:
1. Do you know the purposes of your admission to treatment?
2. Do you have your own purposes for residential treatment?
3. Do the others know what you want to achieve?
4. Are you supported in reaching your personal goals?

The answers to the questions are given by marking one of four possibilities, ranking from very well or very much to hardly or none, and by answering one open question which asks for examples.

1 Do you know the purposes of your admission to treatment.

very well	fairly well	a little	hardly

Specify the purposes you know:

Questions about energy, structure and communication with the surroundings are developed in the same way (the questionnaires can be obtained from the author).

15.7 Making a system analysis and improvement of the social system

A system analysis is necessary to decide upon action for improvement of the system.

I shall give you an example of the way I used the questionnaires while working as a consultant with a team and supporting staff in an institute for abused women and their children. At the first meeting we went through the questionnaire for the workers about conditions for the clients. We went through the questionnaire to see if everybody could understand the questions and the way to work with them. After that the group was divided into pairs to help each other. Each worker filled out the questionnaire for all (10) women. I emphasized that the workers should give their subjective opinion. I always add: 'It does not have to be true or objective. We need your subjective opinion about the way things are'.

After that we tally the responses on the scales for all clients. By listing the scores vertically an image of the conditions for growth and participation as offered by the institute to the clients is presented. See for an example figure 2.

1	Is familiar with treatment goals	10	21	39	30
2	Develops own goals		12	30	58
3	Shares his goals		4	20	76
4	Supports own goals		18	42	40
5	Aware of opportunities	2	12	43	43
6	Has capacities	32	40	28	
7	Capacities are evoked		16	39	45
8	Obstructions are neutralized		2	58	40
9	Exerts influence		2	18	80
10	Influenced by the staff	40	22	20	18
11	Influence on staff		2	40	58
12	Active relationships outside		6	16	78
13	Prepares for after treatment	2	16	30	52

Figure 2   System analysis (10 workers, 10 clients)

The team was asked to draw tentative conclusions and to formulate steps towards improvement. We came to an agreement about action to be undertaken concerning the influence of the women upon daily affairs. The first action aimed at improving the group meeting.

In the second meeting we evaluated the action and decided on further action (This was repeated in every meeting). In this meeting we also went through the questionnaire for the clients. We decided on an adaption of the questionnaire and how to present it to the clients. (The client questionnaire always has to be adapted according to the age, mental and intellectual capacities of the clients).

We decided to have a special group meeting. In the group meeting the women were stimulated to help each other. The questionnaire was translated for two of the women. After the meeting the workers collected the questionnaires.

In the third meeting workers and staff elaborated on a plan to share the results of the questionnaires and the first tentative conclusions with the women.

In the fourth meeting the questionnaire about conditions for the workers was presented. The group was divided into pairs and stimulated to help each other.

The three questionnaires presented a fairly complete insight into the conditions for growth and participation the system offers. Conclusions could be sharpened and more specific action towards improvement could be undertaken. During the consultancy project we constantly:
- evaluated actions undertaken to improve the chosen topic
  (= system characteristic);
- selected new topics to work on;
- incorporated successful actions into the daily routine.

After a while we realized that goal development, utilization of energy, development of structure and communication with the surroundings had improved such that the social climate and participation of both clients and workers was more satisfying. Workers became more conscious of their responsibilities. Clients developed more goals for treatment and could experiment with their capacities to reach their own goals and support each other.

Once working with the social climate was recognized and incorporated as a way of treating clients, the consultancy project could come to an end.

15.8 Finally

In the consultancy project mentioned above, we listed all rankings vertically to come to a system analysis. We can also group the rankings of all workers concerning one client and match these with the rankings of the client himself. This gives an image of the opportunities for growth and participation the institute offers to this particular client, and a useful indication for increasing those opportunities. See for an example figure 3.

1	Is familiar with treatment goals	2	4	4	
2	Develops own goals		2	4	4
3	Shares his goals			4	6
4	Support to own goals			6	4
5	Aware of opportunities		5	2	3
6	Has capacities	3	5	2	
7	Capacities are evoked		1	5	4
8	Obstructions are neutralized			5	5
9	Exerts influence			2	8
10	Influenced by the staff	7	3		
11	Influence upon staff		1	3	6
12	Active relationships outside			2	8
13	Prepares for after treatment			1	9

Figure 3   System conditions for one client

The analysis of the conditions that the institute and the treatment program offer the client to participate in his own treatment and to use his energy to reach his own goals and to support the other clients, has proved to be of great value. It means a shift in focus from diagnosing to empowering.

15.9 Summary

This chapter presents briefly the translation of General System Theory into Social System Theory and its application to residential treatment. The focus is on improving the social climate of the treatment centre and the participation of the clients and workers.
The application of Social System Theory is not restricted to residential treatment, but relevant to all treatment where collaboration with clients and among clients is indispensable.

References

Houweling-Meyer, O., & Visser, K. (1988). *Inrichtingswerk, een systeemgerichte benadering*. Nijmegen: Dekker & Van de Vegt.

Polsky, H.W., & Claster, D.S. (1968). *The dynamics of residential treatment, a social system analysis*. Chapel Hill: University of N. Carolina Press.

Goffman, E. (1961). *Asylums*. New York: Anchor Books, Doubleday & Co.

Parsons, T. (1951). *The social system*. Glencoe: The Free Press.

Buckly, W. (1969), *Modern system research for the behavioural scientist*. Chicago: Aldine Publishing Company.

Luhmann, N. (1988). *Soziale Systeme, Grundrisz einer algemeinen Theorie*. Frankfurt am Main: Suhrkamp.

Visser, K., Bassant, J., & Vernooy, G. (1991). *Methodiekontwikkeling voor de residentiële hulpverlening*. Amsterdam: Hogeschool van Amsterdam.

16   Theoretical and Methodological Developments in Social Policy Research

M. van de Vall

16.1   Problems, theory and methods

16.1.1   Unstructured problems

The term 'social policy research' implies the existence of: (a) a policy problem and: (b) a current or future policy program aimed at reducing that problem. A confusing element in the relationship between problem and program is that policy problems are 'unstructured'. Compared to problems in applied physical science, for instance, problems in applied social science are called 'sick': From a science point of view, policy problems are sick problems. What is meant is that from the point of view of research, policy problems are hard to operationalize, due to the following factors: double complexity, a latent as well as a manifest structure and a multiplicity of meanings.

Double complexity. From the point of view of policy making, policy problems consist of conditions, interests, values, symbols and perceptions, some of which are manipulable while others are not. From the point of view of research, however, policy problems consist of a variety of variables: antecedent, independent, intervening and dependent variables, unintended and latent variables. Translating the first complexity in terms of the second will often take several months.

Latent and manifest structure. Manifest problem behaviour is often a symptom of underlying social structures and latent individual needs: Strike behaviour may express work dissatisfaction, crime behaviour may be caused by drug addiction, urban riots as a response to racial discrimination. In addition, one type of problem behavior, e.g. vandalism, may be caused by different conditions and different needs. Policymakers, by the way, are often more inclined to treat the symptoms than improve the conditions.

Multiple meanings. In most policy problems, several stakeholders are involved. In juvenile crime, for instance: the police force, lawyers, DA's, judges, journalists, criminals, probation officers, social workers, prison guards and victims. Although new methods of stakeholder analysis provide an in-depth description of the various perceptions, choosing one of those perceptions as a criterion for program impact is rather a matter of politics than of research.

Confronted with the complicated task of diagnosing the unstructured relationship between policy problems and programs, social policy research has responded with methodological and theoretical developments. A methodological development, for instance, is the use of 'triangulated' research designs. In a triangulated design, methods from different epistemological paradigms are combined in *one* project of policy research. A theoretical development is the growing use of 'operational' theory, for instance the construction of 'heuristic' multivariate models in a graphic form. We shall discuss those developments below.

16.1.2 *Triangulated methods*
In social policy research, using 'mixed' methods is accompanied by higher rates of utilization than the use of single-method designs (Van de Vall, Bolas & Kang, 1976; 173). This is reflected in a growing popularity of triangulation in applied social science. In a review of projects of social policy research in The Netherlands and the United States (no representative sample) we encountered three different modes of triangulation.

a. *Methodological triangulation.* Quantitative methods of data collecting and analysis are combined with qualitative methods. In program evaluation, for instance, the quantitative method of impact measurement is combined with the qualitative method of program monitoring (Rossi & Freeman, 1989; chapter 4).

b. *Strategic triangulation.* Bottom-up strategies are combined with top-down strategies of social policy research. For instance, both the con-

201

sumers and the providers of agency services are included in the assessment of a policy program (Ham & Hill, 1986).

c. *Paradigmatic triangulation.* Investigative methods of program evaluation are combined with formative methods of policy intervention (O'Shaugnessy, 1972). Thus, empirical analysis and policy recommendations are integrated in the professional role of the policy consultant.

In the third category, of paradigmatic triangulation, the epistemological values of social science research merge with the implemental values of knowledge utilization. This is a tricky task. In fact, creating a 'satisfycing' integration between epistemological and implemental values is probably one of the most difficult methodological problems in social policy research (Van de Vall, 1987).

16.1.3 Conceptual models
Working in a cognitive 'no mans's land' between concrete facts and abstract theory, policy researchers are in need of middle-range operational concepts that will assist them in designing a problem reducing policy program. In his answer to this need, Gordon Lippitt in 1973 introduced the heuristic instrument of graphic conceptual models. An organizational consultant, Lippitt had discovered the advantages of graphic conceptual models in analyzing unstructured policy problems. A few years later, Harrell Allen (1978) discovered graphic conceptual models to operate as 'Gestalt communication modes' in the interaction between policy researchers and the client system.

Yet, even after 20 years, relatively little is known about the procedure of constructing multivariate conceptual models. According to Strauss (1987; chapter 8), the researcher "wallows, suffers and agonizes" over his or her data, gradually forcing them into increasingly complicated conceptual diagrams. In this procedure, intuitive 'Verstehen' goes hand in hand with more systematic procedures of analytic reduction. In social policy research, using graphic conceptual models has the following advantages.

a. *Comprehensive reduction of the policy problem.* Translating a problem in terms of a conceptual model results in a reduced as well as a comprehensive ('Gestalt') diagnosis, presenting major elements of the problem in the context of a functional relationship with the policy program.

b. *Dynamic analysis of the policy problem*. Translating a policy problem in terms of independent and dependent variables emphasizes the dynamic relationship between program and problem. In the resulting model, the dependent variable is usually operationalized in terms of measurable indicators.

c. *Manipulability of the policy problem*. Policymakers are mainly interested in the manipulability of discriminating variables. Using a conceptual model, manipulable variables can be distinguished from the non-manipulable ones. Often, the kind of the manipulation (coercion, persuasion, punishment, rewards, etc.) is also indicated.

Conceptual models carry various names in social policy research: 'skeletal structures' (Harre, 1976), 'frames' (Stein & Schon, 1986), 'integrative diagrams' (Strauss, 1987), 'template structures' (Harre, 1979), 'dynamic flow chart models' (Lippitt, 1973), 'conceptual maps' (Finsterbusch & Motz, 1980) and 'multiple pictures of the world by multiple stakeholders' (Mitroff, 1985). This confusion notwithstanding, social policy researchers increasingly use conceptual models for the following purposes: (a) the *ex ante* design of a policy program, (b) the *current* monitoring of program implementation, and (c) the *ex post* evaluation of a policy program.

In clinical evaluation, improving the program is part of the method.

16.2 The two developments illustrated: clinical program evaluation

In the remainder of this chapter, triangulation and conceptual modelling will be illustrated at a 'clinical' method of program evaluation and adjustment. In this clinical design of program evaluation, three methods of research and intervention are combined in one project:

(A) Impact evaluation: Using quantitative impact indicators, it is measured whether a policy program, in its unique execution at a particular time and location, is accompanied by a significant reduction of problem behavior (Campbell, 1986).

(B) *Process evaluation*: Using conceptual models of policy implementation, it is assessed which elements in the execution of the program are responsible for a less than optimal rate of impact.

(C) *Formative evaluation*: Using interaction between researcher and client, recommendations are formulated about the relationship between program and problem that will result in higher impact.

From the point of view of improving the program, the three methods *complement* each other. Bottom-up method A (impact measurement) produces quantitative information about the reduction of problem behavior. Top-down method B (program monitoring) provides qualitative data about the resources, environment and implementation of the program. Using data from A and B, formative method C (policy intervention) formulates suggestions for strengthening the program. The triangulation of methods A, B and C into one comprehensive project of program evaluation and adjustment is illustrated in figure 1:

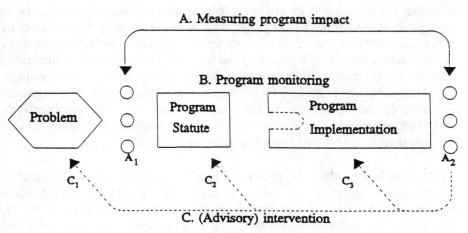

Figure 1   *A Triangulated Case Method of Program Evaluation and Adjustment*

Over a period of ten years, this 'clinical' design of program evaluation has been applied to a large number of policy programs in industrial companies, business firms and public institutions in Europe and United States. The three triangulated methods are discussed in the next sections.

16.3 Summative evaluation: impact measurement (A)

A central activity in policy evaluation is measuring valid indicators of the problem, before and after implementation of the program. In the clinical design, this is based upon the assumption of double validity, i.e. of the indicators being both epistemologically *and* implementally valid. In other words, they shall not only measure what they are supposed to measure, but also enable the researcher to improve the evaluated policy program (Brinkerhoff & Dressler, 1990; 113).

Meeting the standards of epistemological *and* implemental validity is complicated by the fact that program goals are usually formulated in terms of abstract, categorical concepts, e.g. happiness, democracy, justice, education, social equality, safety, etc. In program evaluation, however, empirical, continuous concepts are used, e.g. 'Percentage juveniles having completed the local drug rehabilitation program'. The discrepancy between the abstract language of program objectives and the empirical concepts of program evaluation represents a serious threat to the validity of impact indicators.

Operationalizing abstract program goals in terms of a measurable impact-index takes place in a sequence of translations. At each translation, the validity of the indicators is in danger (Hage, 1972). The crises in validity accompanying this process are illustrated in Case One.

Case One: A federal minority emancipation program in the United States. In this case the abstract program goal 'minority emancipation' is translated in terms of a measurable, multiple-item emancipation index, shown in figure 2.

MINORITY EMANCIPATION

1. Nominal definition: Equality in matters of: (a) civic rights, (b) political rights, and (c) economic treatment.

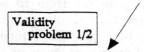

Validity problem 1/2

2. Linear definition: Degree of equal treatment regarding: (a) civic rights, (b) political rights, (c) economic matters.

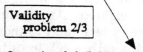

Validity problem 2/3

3. Operational definition: Degree of equality in: (a) Access to education, (b) passive and active election rights, and (c) wages, salary and property.

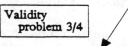

Validity problem 3/4

4. Social indicators:
   Sub (a): Percentage students in high school and universities of the minority group compared with those percentages of the majority group.

   Sub (b): Percentage of elected officials in local, state and national legislative bodies of the minority group, compared with those percentages of the majority group.

   Sub (c): The income distribution in the minority group, in quintiles of GNP, compared with the income distribution in the majority group.

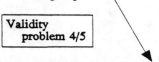

Validity problem 4/5

5. Emancipation index: $\dfrac{1(a)+2(b)+3(c)}{6}$ or $\dfrac{3(a)+2(b)+1(c)}{6}$ or $\dfrac{1(a)+1(b)+1(c)}{3}$

Figure 2   *Validity Problems in Measuring Program Impact: An Illustration*

Figure 2 illustrates how in social policy research, the validity of the indicators is often threatened by a lack of information. At Step 3/4 in figure 2, for instance, problems of data collecting force the researcher to reduce (3b): equality in passive and active election rights, to (4b): the passive right of being elected, dropping the right to elect. For similar reasons, with data about property hard to obtain, (3c): - wage, salary and property, was reduced to (4c): per capita income, dropping property from the index. In both instances, lack of data threatens the content validity of the measuring instrument, a frequent problem in the real world of program evaluation.

We encounter a different threat to validity at Step 4/5 in figure 2, when the three items of the index are weighted. Arguments in favour of formula (3a + 2b + 1c) are no more or less valid to those in favour of (1a + 2b + 3c) or, for that matter, (1a + 1b + 1c). In order to avoid conflicts with the client system after reporting, evaluators often use all three formulas, followed by a dialogue with the stakeholders about the consequences of each formula for policy decisions.

In the clinical evaluation design, *measuring program impact* (A in figure 1) is accompanied by *program monitoring* (B in figure 1). Why is this the case? Rossi and Freeman (1989) provide the answer: 'A large proportion of programs that fail to show impact are really failures to deliver the intervention in ways specified'. This observation is confirmed by Baier, March and Saetren (1990): In the transition from adopting programs to executing policy programs they encountered a number of 'impeding variables' in program implementation.[1] In other words, low program impact is often due to deficient program implementation. This explains why the methods A and B in figure 1 are combined.

---

[1] A striking example: 'Even a causal inspection of many of the projects launched under the Model Cities Program of the 1960s, for instance, revealed that a number of programs for which funds were allocated were never actually implemented.' (Berk et al., 1985, pp. 410-411).

16.4 Process evaluation: program monitoring (B)

While in summative evaluation a problem is measured at two points in time (A1 and A2 in figure 1) and the program treated as a static input-output machine (Deutscher & Beattie, 1988), this is different in process evaluation. Now the program is viewed as dynamic, i.e. as a process of putting a policy into practice. This implementation process is systematically analyzed in method B: program monitoring.

In program monitoring we are confronted with a new epistemological problem, i.e. of the replicability of qualitative case analysis (Hersen & Barlow, 1976). Compared with other methods, for instance, e.g. the experiment and the survey, qualitative case analysis is found to be weak on reliability: neither the single case design nor the multiple case design guarantee that different evaluators will collect similar data, develop similar categories or interpret results from the same theoretical perspective. In an effort to strengthen the reliability of qualitative case research, Yin (1984) recommends the following devices:
a. A case study data base, containing primary and secondary data sources, case study notes, documents, researcher's work books, code-books, tabular material and narratives.
b. A case study protocol, containing an overview of the project, its history, relevant readings, issues investigated, field procedures, questions reflecting the inquiry and a guide for reporting.

There is little doubt that use of a data base and a protocol will indeed strengthen the so-called 'instrument' reliability of case analysis, ensuring that the same data are collected and that the same categories are used. The two devices have little effect, however, upon the 'interpretative' reliability of the analysis, as researchers still remain free to explain the findings from different theoretical perspectives.[1]

---

[1] For the distinction between 'instrument' and 'observer' reliability, see: Behling & Merves, 1984. In our text, their term 'observer' reliability used by Behling and Merves has been renamed in 'interpretative' reliability.

Thus, even with data base and protocol, the interpretative reliability of the case study remains low.

To strengthen the interpretative reliability of the case method of program monitoring, a different, more abstract device is required: A theoretical framework that will enable researchers to analyze a body of data from a similar theoretical perspective. Because of the 'unstructured' character of policy problems, this framework should consist of one or more multivariate conceptual models of program implementation (Scheirer, 1981). Following Scriven (1974) and Mohr (1985) we have called this procedure: 'systemic modus operandi' (SMO). For use in program monitoring, three different conceptual models of program implementation were selected from the literature:
1. A statutory model (Sabatier & Mazmanian, 1980);
2. A context model (Mayer & Greenwood, 1980); and
3. A trajectory model (Harrell Allen, 1978).
Together, the three models cover the process of policy implementation. Use of the models standardizes the procedures of data collecting and analysis in case study research. In the context of policy research, the interpretative reliability of the case method of program monitoring is strengthened. We shall now discuss each of the conceptual models.

16.4.1 A statutory model of program implementation
In a theoretical framework of policy making, Sabatier and Mazmanian (1980) present twenty-two variables affecting program implementation.[1] Seven of those variables are 'statutory' variables, i.e formulated in the bylaws, the statute or the charter of the program. Operating as the program's statutory foundation, they lend direction and coherence to the complicated process of program implementation. The seven statutory variables fall into three categories: Policy variables, instrumental variables and resource variables, shown in figure 3.

---

[1] The Sabatier and Mazmanian (1980) model has been validated, among others, by Vosburgh (1986).

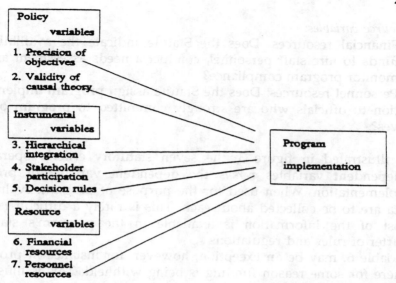

Figure 3   *The Relationship between 'Statutory' Variables and Program Implementation*

Policy variables:
1. Precision of objectives: Does the program Statute provide clearly ranked instructions for agency and target group how to conform to program objectives?
2. Validity of causal theory: Does the program Statute indicate how the implementing agencies will produce the planned change in the target group?

Instrumental variables:
3. Hierarchical integration: Does the program Statute create an integrated hierarchical network of implementing agencies?
4. Stakeholder participation: Does the program Statute provide liberal rules to participation in decisions by stakeholders committed to the program?
5. Decision rules: Does the program Statute stipulate how the decision regulations of implementing agencies support the program goal?

210

Resource variables:
6. Financial resources: Does the Statute indicate the availibility of funds to hire staff personnel, conduct a needs assessment and/or monitor program compliance?
7. Personnel resources: Does the Statute assign program implementation to officials who are strongly committed to program objectives?

As illustrated in figure 3, the seven statutory criteria operate as independent variables *versus* the dependent variable of program implementation. When used for the purpose of program evaluation, data are to be collected about each. This is rarely a difficult task, as most of the information is available in the program's statutory charter of rules and regulations.

Variable 6. may be an exception, however, for instance in programs where for some reason funding is being withheld. This is illustrated in Case Two.

Case Two: Women's Job Corps. Thompson (1978) describes: 'The rare case of a federal agency which for its sustenance was dependent upon a number of voluntary organizations, state organizations and other organizations such as the AFL-CIO. The Women's Job Corps was approved by Congress like most other federal agencies but with one outstanding difference: Unlike most federal agencies the Women's Job Corps did not have an officially approved budget.'

Although the answers to the seven questions in the model (figure 3) are indicative for the policymaker's commitment to careful implementation of the program, positive scores on all seven criteria will not automatically guarantee high program impact. This is mainly due to a number of 'constraint' variables in the strategic environment of the program. They are described in the next section.

16.4.2 A context model of program implementation
The context model consists of nine variables constituting the strategic environment of program implementation (Mayer & Greenwood, 1981). Core of the model is the relationship between the independent variable 'statute of the program' and the dependent variable 'program impact'. Located between these two are the intervening variable

'program implementation' and a so-called 'bridging' variable. The latter is a non-manipulable precondition for attaining the program goal, for instance the ability to read and write in a locally funded computer course for unemployed workers.

The four core variables are surrounded by adjunct, constraint and secondary variables. An *adjunct variable* is a supplementary measure supporting goal attainment, e.g. travel reimbursement for participants living outside a circle of 30 miles from the place where the computer course is given. *Constraint variables* are: (a) Conditions in the program's environment and: (b) Characteristics of the target group. There are also two types of *secondary impact*: (a) Unintended effect of introducing the program, e.g. protest from applicants excluded from the program, and: (b) Latent effects of attaining the program goal, e.g. tax loss due to the fact that graduates find employment outside the funding community.

The nine variables are interrelated in a causal pattern, illustrated in figure 4 (Mayer & Greenwood op. cit.).

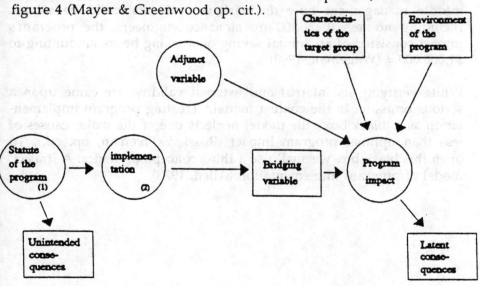

(1) Evaluated with the 'statutory' model of implementation (Sabatier & Mazmanian, 1980)
(2) Evaluated with the 'trajectory' model of implementation (Harrel Allen, 1978)

○ Manipulable variable
□ Non-manipulable variable

Figure 4   *The 'Contextual' Model of Program Implementation (Mayer & Greenwood, 1980)*

As most other conceptual models in the social sciences, the context model is a 'heuristic', i.e. its structure can be adjusted to different environments. This flexibility is illustrated in Case Three, reported by a Dutch organization consultant.

Case three: 'Take car home' program. In firm X (electrical system maintenance) a 'take car home' program has been introduced for use of 120 company service cars. Instead of daily picking up a car at the central office, the engineers now take the car home. Each morning they directly drive to the job site of that day. Elimination of the daily visits to central office, however, required a number of technical and organizational adaptations from middle-management. Explaining the *ex ante* policy, the program evaluator used the following version of the context model.
Using an overhead presentation of figure 5 as a 'Gestalt communication mode' (Allen, op. cit.) the evaluator succeeded in convincing middle management how the various problems could be solved. Including no less than 200 maintenance engineers, the program's impact consisted of an annual saving of working hours amounting to $1,000.000.= (Wageman, 1990).

While verifying its internal and external validity, we came upon a serious omission in the context model.[1] Treating program implementation as a 'black box', the model neglects one of the major causes of less than optimal program impact (Rossi & Freeman, op. cit.). To open this black box we shall use a third conceptual device: A 'traject' model of program implementation (Allen, 1978).

---

[1] The pragmatic validity of the context and the traject models has been verified in more than 100 cases of program monitoring by graduate students in a seminar on 'Organizational Analysis and Program Assessment' at SUNY/Buffalo and the Erasmus University, Rotterdam, The Netherlands.

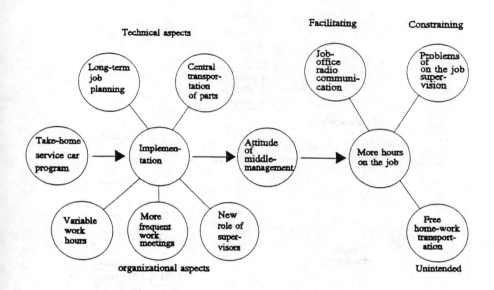

Figure 5　　Main features of a 'take home service car' program in an electrical system maintenance firm

16.4.3 A traject model of program implementation

An efficient theoretical instrument for analyzing program implementation is the Delta chart, constructed by Harrel Allen (1978). This algorithm type process model is constructed with an IBM flowchart template or, more sophisticatedly, with a graphic computer program. The Delta chart enables the evaluator to analyze program implementation from the first stage: an external incident triggering program operation, to the last stage: program output.[1]

The Delta chart is constructed with five graphic symbols: 1. Decision box; 2. Event box; 3. Logic box; 4. Time arrow; 5. Activity box (acronym DELTA). The basic type of Delta model is shown in figure 6. Each of the five symbols in the model will be explained.

---

[1] For a more detailed description of the Delta model, see Harrell Allen (1978).

214

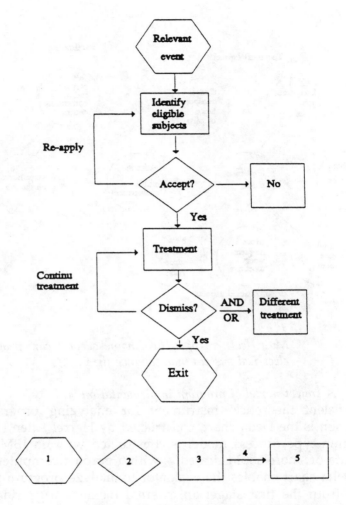

Figure 6   *Algorithm (Delta chart) of Program Implementation*

1. The *event* box stands for an external event triggering program activity, but not involving any time or work within the program. Examples are: 'Apprehension' in a detention program, 'initiative' in an innovation program, 'application' in a training program, 'offense' in a drug testing program, 'illness' in a program caring for the sick, etc.

2. The *decision* box (diamond) indicates that, after completion of a step in the program, a new decision has to be made. The alternatives are: Yes, continue to the next step; No, reject subject (client, trainee, inmate, etc.) from the program; Redo, revise previous activity using a feedback route.
3. The *logic* box represents a consequence or function of the preceding step: *And* indicates additional activities, e.g. therapy in addition to training; *Or* indicates transfer to a substitute activity, e.g. therapy instead of training.
4. The *time* arrow symbolizes the program's trajectory over time, with one exception: Related to a decision diamond, it indicates the logical consequences of: Yes, No or Redo, described in 2.
5. The *activity* box indicates a specific program task, e.g.: counselling, supervising, testing, rendering a service, writing a prescription, teaching a course, conducting therapy, providing assistance, etc.

Because it compels evaluators to view implementation from the same perspective, i.e. as a sequence of decisions toward goal realization, the Delta model is an additional device to strengthen the 'interpretative' reliability of the qualitative case method of program monitoring. A more practical benefit results when Delta is used for formative purposes. In this application, the model is constructed and discussed with the active participation from the field officers implementing the program. Individual idiosyncrasies in the choice of criteria for decisions and differences in program treatment are articulated, discussed and, where necessary, corrected. An example of this type of formative evaluation is Case Eight, described in the next section.

16.5 Formative evaluation: adjusting the program (C)

After the impact of the program has been measured (method A) and its implementation monitored (method B), clients usually ask for advice about ways of improving the program. Providing those recommendations and assisting the client system in their adoption and realization (method C), is an important activity in clinical program evaluation.
This shift from evaluation to intervention is accompanied by a differentiation of underlying values. More specifically, the epistemological

standards of evaluation research are now accompanied by the instrumental values of policy design or improvement and, ultimately, by
the values of planned innovation (Fischhoff, 1987). The conclusion is
that with moving to method C, the values expressed in the program's goals become part of the clinical method of program evaluation.

However, working with a double set of values, epistemological and
ideological, will enhance the chances of conflict between the
evaluator and the client, especially when research results are transformed into policy action. Preventing this conflict requires a climate
of trust between the researcher and the client (Kash & Ballard, 1987;
607; Van de Vall, 1987).[1] Creating this climate is mainly the responsibility of the researcher. Once this is established, the recommendations fall into the following categories: 1. Redefining the policy
problem (C1 in figure 1); 2. Reformulating the program statute (C2);
3. Revising program implementation (C3). The three categories are
discussed in the next section.

16.5.1 Redefining the policy problem (C1)

In social policy research, definitions of the problem often change in
the course of one research project. With each new conceptual model,
for instance, the evaluator changes his perspective and his or her
definition of the problem is adjusted. Also, new questions are formulated and different data have to be collected. Illustrations of this
practice of problem redefinition are:

Case four: Increasing union membership. The problem 'Why is the membership of union X declining?' was first redefined as: 'What are the
benefits of union membership for individual members'? and second
as: 'How can individual grievance solving by union X be improved?'

---

[1] In program evaluation, communication and trust can be enhanced if the conceptual models are used in a context of process-oriented organizational diagnosis. In
this process: '..the studies become part of the policymaking process while they are
being carried out' (Kash & Ballard, Op. cit.; 608). For this method, see also Bartee
and Cheyunski (1977).

Subsequent action research resulted in a number of policy recommendations.[1]

Case five: Facilitating industrial innovation. The problem 'How can innovation in small and medium-sized firms be promoted?' was redefined first as: 'How can the firms cope with information overload?', and second as: 'How can the firms cope with information underuse?' (Van de Vall, 1983). Research about the last two questions resulted in the removal of several barriers to innovation.

Case six: Controlling urban crime. The problem 'How can the small crime rate in city X be reduced?' was redefined first as: 'How can local police in X contribute to crime control?', second as: 'Does traffic control leave local police time for crime control?' and finally as: 'In crime control by local police, should priority be given to: (a) obtaining many convictions, using short interrogations of many suspects, or to (b) solving many cases, using in-depth interrogations of fewer suspects?'[2]

In each of those cases, redefining the problem resulted in greater specification of the relationship between program and problem. Thus, with each redefinition, a step was made toward reduction of the problem. A disadvantage of this procedure is, however, is that with each redefinition, new data about the problem and\or the program have to be collected and, sometimes, another method of analysis is called for. Together, the procedures of redefining the problem, operationalizing the new version and triangulating several methods are essential features of clinical program evaluation.

---

[1] For a more detailed analysis of this problem: Van de Vall (1970, chapter 4 and 6).

[2] The author has for several years served as a research consultant on a National advisory board on urban crime control of the Netherlands' Ministries of Justice and Internal Affairs.

16.5.2 Reformulating the program Statute (C2)
When a policy program is drafted, latent assumptions of stakeholders, e.g. about ways of reducing the problem, are reflected in the statute of rules and regulations. Many of those cause-effect assumptions are not only latent, however, but also hypothetical and untested. Systematically articulating those assumptions and correcting the non-valid ones has a triple effect upon the program: It improves the statute of the program, strengthens implementation and, indirectly, increases program impact.
This method of 'assumption analysis' consists of several steps:
(a) *Specifying stakeholders*: Various stakeholders are identified and their relationship to the program (consumer, provider, sponsor, etc.) is established;
(b) *Articulating assumptions*: Stakeholders' goals, assumptions and expectations about the Program are articulated, using primary and secondary information;
(c) *Constructing policy theory*: The assumptions sub (b) are formulated in a logical structure of 'if-then' propositions, and coordinated in a logically coherent theoretical system: the policy theory.
(d) *Assessing policy theory*: The empirical, theoretical and implemental quality of the policy theory sub (c) is evaluated, using epistemological, implemental and/or strategic criteria.[1]
(e) *Adjusting the Statute*: In iterative communication with stakeholders, the way incorrect or unfeasible assumptions are reflected in the program statute is corrected.

Methods of assumption analysis are used increasingly in social policy research. Examples are: Company management science (Mason & Mitroff, 1981), product marketing (Zaltman, Lemasters & Heffring, 1982), social welfare and administration (Elkin & Vorwaller, 1975), public administration (Fischer, 1980), public education policy (Hoeben, 1989), family and population policy (Leeuw & Van de Vall, 1984), public information (McGuire, 1981; Gageldonk, Leeuw & Dekker, 1987).
Case Seven is an example of assumption analysis in the area of public information:

---

[1] For a systematic presentation of these criteria: Van de Vall (1987).

Case seven: A public information campaign. After completing a public information campaign about changes in the social security system, the Dutch government asked Leeuw to evaluate the campaign's underlying assumptions. The evaluator reformulated the assumptions in terms of a 'persuasion theory' of causal statements. The quality of each statement was tested against available social science information. Two assumptions were corrected: (a) Widespread civil disobedience had not been prevented: the expectations had been unfounded; (b) Free rider behavior had not been eradicated, this having been too widespread in the target population (Leeuw, 1988).

16.5.3 Revising program implementation (C3)

At the third stage of formative evaluation (C3 in figure 1), the recommendations take the form of suggestions for planned change, or policy innovation. The recommended changes vary from incremental, e.g. gradually correcting implementation (*ex post*), to synoptic, e.g. designing a new or different program (*ex ante*).
Case Eight is an example of incremental program change in a municipal welfare agency:

Case eight: Uniformity of treatment. In Agency X, the case officers' discretionary decisions showed considerable differences, resulting in inequality of treatment. After drafting a Delta chart of the process of implementation, the evaluator compared the criteria used by case officers at each 'decision diamond' in the model. This resulted in greater uniformity in decisions about: (a) adopting new clients, (b) disbursing treatment (c) dismissing clients from the program.

In comparison, synoptic recommendations require not only a more extensive preparation from the evaluator, but also a more comprehensive design of the program and, above all, a tolerance in the client system of radical innovation. In *ex ante* policy design, the three conceptual models of program implementation (statutory, context, trajectory) are applied to drafting a new or entirely different policy program.
This is illustrated in Case Nine.

Case nine: A new grievance solving procedure. Investigating existing practices of individual grievance solving in total institutions (hospitals, prisons) in The Netherlands, Mante-Meijer (1989) designed an 'optimal' grievance solving procedure in total institutions that resulted in: (a) easier access to the grievance system, (b) more effective treatment of the grievance, (c) follow-up procedures after grievance resolution. The innovation is widely adopted.

16.6 Conclusion

Clinical program evaluation is in more than one respect based upon a multi-paradigmatic approach. First, because it covers both consumers and providers of the evaluated program. Second, because quantitative methods of impact measurement are combined with qualitative methods of program monitoring. Thirdly, because methods of policy research are integrated with methods of policy intervention.

Each method is coping with its own, specific problem. In impact measurement (A in figure 1) it is the validity of the impact indicators. In the case method of program monitoring (B in figure 1) the problem is the reliability of the observations. In formative evaluation (C in figure 1) the problem it predominantly strategic: Creating of a climate of communication and trust between researcher and client.

The simultaneous solution of those epistemological *and* implemental problems is one of the most neglected assignments in program evaluation.

References

Allen, T.H. (1978). *New methods in social science research*. New York: Praeger.

Argyris, C., Putnam R., & McLain Smith, D. (1985). *Action science; concepts, methods and skills for research and intervention*. San Francisco: Jossey Bass.

Baier, V.E., March, J.G. & Saetren, H. (1990). Implementation and ambiguity. In: J.G. March [ed.], *Decisions and organizations* (pp. 150-164). Oxford: Basil Blackwell.

Bartee, E.M., & Cheyunski, F. (1977). A methodology for process oriented organizational diagnosis. *The Journal of Applied Behavioral Science, 13*, 153-68.

Berk, R.A., et al. (1985). Social policy experimentation: a position paper. *Evaluation Review, 9*, 387-429.

Brinkerhoff, R.O., & Dressler, D.E. (1990). *Productivity measurement.* Beverly Hills: Sage.

Campbell, D.T. (1986). Relabelling internal and external validity for applied social scientists. In W.M.K. Trochim [ed.], *Advances in quasi experimental design and analysis* (p. 69). San Francisco: Jossey Bass.

Checkland, P., & Scholes, J. (1990). *Soft systems methodology in action.* New York: Wiley and Sons.

Davidson, W.S, Redner, R., & Saul, J.A. (1985). Research modes in social and community change. In E. Seidman [ed.], *Handbook of social intervention* (pp. 99-118). Beverly Hills: Sage.

Deutscher, I., & Beattie, M. (1988). Success and failure: static concepts in a dynamic society. *Evaluation Review, 12*, 607-624.

Dunn, W.N. (1981). *Public policy analysis.* Englewood Cliffs: Prentice Hall.

Elkin, R., & Vorwaller, D. (1975). Evaluating the effectiveness of social services. In L. Seidler & E. Seidler [Eds.], *Social accounting: theory, issues and cases* (pp. 410-426). Los Angeles: Academic Press.

Fischer, (1980). *Politics, values and public policy: the problem of methodology.* Boulder.

Fischhoff, B. (1986). Clinical policy analysis. In W.N. Dunn [ed.], *Policy analysis: perspectives, concepts and problems* (pp. 111-130). Greenwich: Conn. JAI Press.

Gageldonk, A. van, Leeuw, F., & Dekker, P. (1987). Analyse van voorlichtings-veronderstellingen. *Massacommunicatie, 15*, 175-191.

Hage, J. (1972). *Techniques and problems of theory construction in sociology.* New York: Wiley.

Ham, C., & Hill, M. (1986). *The policy process in the modern capitalist state.* Bighton.

Harre, R. (1976). The constructive role of models. In L. Collins [ed.], *The use of models in social science* (pp. 16-43). London: Tavistock.

Harre, R. (1979). *Social Being.* London: Basil Blackwell.

Harrell Allen, T. (1978). *New methods in the social sciences.* New York: Preager.

222

Hersen, M., & Barlow, D.H. (1976). *Single case experimental designs: strategies for studying behavior change*. New York: Pergamon Press.

Hoaglin, D., Light, R.J., McPeek, B., Mosteller, F., & Stoto, M.A. (1982). *Data for decisions*. Cambridge (MA): Abt.

Hoeben, W.T.J.G. (1989). Dansen om de regenboom. *Nederlands Tijdschrift voor Opvoeding, Vorming en Onderwijs*, 5, 28-40.

Kash, D.E., & Ballard, S. (1987) Academic and applied policy studies. *The American Behavioral Scientist*, 30, 597-611.

Leeuw, F.L., & Van de Vall, M. (1984). National population policies in industrial countries: praxis or paradox? In R.F. Tomasson [ed.], *Comparative Social Research*, 7, 351-368.

Leeuw, F.L. (1988). Overheidsvoorlichting en de wijziging van het sociale zekerheidsstelsel. *Beleid en Maatschappij*, 1, 20-44.

Leeuw, F.L. (1990). Analyzing policy theories and the systematic use of knowledge for public policy In B. Guy Peters & T.A. Barker [eds.], *Advice to governments*. London/Berkeley: Sage.

Lippitt, G. (1973). *Visualizing change: model building and the change process*. La Jolla: University Associates.

Mante-Meijer, E. (1989). *Conflicten in organisaties; individuele klachten en hun behandeling*. Rotterdam: Risbo Press.

Mason, R.O., & Mitroff, I.I. (1981). *Challenging strategic planning assumptions*. New York: Wiley.

Mayer, R., & Greenwood, E. (1980). *The design of social policy research*. Englewood Cliffs: Prentice Hall.

McGuire, W.J. (1981). Theoretical foundations of campaigns. In R.E. Rice & W.J. Paisley [eds.], *Public communication campaigns* (ch. 2). Beverly Hills\London: Sage.

Mitroff, I.I. (1985). Why our old pictures of the world do not work any more. In E.E. Lawler III, et al. [eds.], *Doing research that is useful for theory and practice* (pp. 118-136). San Francisco: Jossey-Bass.

Mohr, L.B. (1985). The reliability of the case study as a source of information. In R.F. Coulam & R.A. Smith [eds.], *Advances in information processing in organizations*. Greenwich: JAI Press.

O'Shaugnessy, J. (1972). *Inquiry and decision*. London: Allen & Unwin.

Ravetz, J.R. (1987). Usable knowledge, usable ignorance: incomplete science with policy implications. *Knowledge: Creation, Diffusion, Utilization*, 9, 86-116.

Rossi, P.H., & Freeman, H. (1989). *Evaluation, a systematic approach.* Beverly Hills: Sage (fourth ed.).

Sabatier, P., & Mazmanian, D. (1980). The implementation of public policy: a framework of analysis. *Policy Studies, Special Issue: Symposium on Successful Policy Implementation,* 538-559.

Scheirer, M.A. (1981). *Program implementation, a framework of analysis.* Beverly Hills: Sage.

Scriven, M. (1974). Maximizing the power of causal investigations: the modus operandi method. In W.J. Popham [ed.], *Evaluation in education; current applications* (pp. 68-84). Berkeley: McCutchan.

Stein, M., & Schon, A. (1986). Frame reflective discourse. *Beleidsanalyse, 15,* 4, 4-18.

Strauss, A.L. (1987). *Qualitative analysis for social scientists.* Cambridge: Cambridge University Press.

Thompson, M.M. (1978). *A study of interorganizational coordination: the Organization-Set Example* (unpublished Ph D. dissertation). SUNY/-Buffalo.

Van de Vall, M. (1970). *Labour organizations; a macro- and micro-sociological analysis on a comparative basis.* Cambridge: Cambridge University Press.

Van de Vall, M. (1987). Data based sociological practice: a professional paradigm. *The American Behavioral Scientist, 30,* 644-660.

Van de Vall, M., Bolas, C., & Kang, T.S. (1976). Applied social research in industrial organizations. *The Journal of Applied Behavioral Science, 11,* 114-138.

Vosburgh, M. (1986). Implementation analysis: a case of accident compensation in New Zealand. *Evaluation and Program Planning, 9,* 49-59.

Wageman, A. (1990). *Report about the GEB research 'take home' project* (personal correspondence with the author).

Yin, R.K. (1984). *Case study research; design and methods.* Beverly Hills: Sage.

Zaltman, G., Lemasters, K., & Heffring, M. (1982). *Theory construction in marketing: some thoughts on thinking.* New York: Wiley.

CONTRIBUTORS

P.M. van den Bergh. Lecturer at the Department of Education, Leiden University.

Centre for Special Education and Child Care
P.O. Box 9555
2300 RB Leiden,
The Netherlands.

D.G. Challender. Staff Consultant at the 'Caldecott Community' in Ashford, Kent.

The Caldecott Community
Mersham Le Hatch
Ashford,
Kent TN 25 5 NH,
United Kingdom.

P.L.M. van der Doef. Psychologist and Treatment Co-ordinator at the 'Paedologisch Instituut' in Nijmegen.

Paedologisch Instituut
Hengstdal 3
6522 JV Nijmegen,
The Netherlands.

P. Durning. Professor at the Laboratoire Éducation et Formation, Université Paris X - Nanterre.

Laboratoire Éducation et Formation
200 Avenue de la République
92001 Nanterre,
France.

F.M. Edens. Researcher at the Department of Personality and Educational Psychology, University of Groningen.

Personality and Educational Psychology. Psychologisch Instituut Heymans
Grote Kruisstraat 2-1
9712 TS Groningen,
The Netherlands.

T.P. Keulen. Assistant Director of the 'Stichting Haagse Hervormde Kindertehuizen' in The Hague.

Stichting Haagse Hervormde Kindertehuizen
Duinweg 17a
2585 JT The Hague,
The Netherlands.

M. Klomp. Lecturer at the Department of Education, Leiden University.

Centre for Special Education and Child Care
P.O. Box 9555
2300 RB Leiden,
The Netherlands.

P.H. van der Laan. Project manager for youth research and research in the field of alternative sanctions for both juveniles and adults.

Research and Documentation Centre
Ministry of Justice
Postbus 20301
2500 EH The Hague
The Netherlands.

F.A.E. Pannekoek. He is involved in psychological examination and counselling of young adolescents, and advancement of know how in a residential treatment centre for adolescents.

Orthopedagogisch centrum 'De Amerberg'(U.J.L.)
Emmalaan 18
3818 GG Amersfoort,
The Netherlands.

N.W. Slot. Director of research at the 'Paedologisch Instituut' in Amsterdam/Duivendrecht.

Paedologisch Instituut
P.O. Box 303
1115 ZG Duivendrecht,
The Netherlands.

E.J. Knorth. Lecturer at the Department of Education, Leiden University.

Centre for Special Education and Child Care
P.O. Box 9555
2300 RB Leiden,
The Netherlands.

H. van Loon. Child and adolescent psychiatrist at the child and adolescent psychiatric clinic, Sophia Children's Hospital, Erasmus University.

Child and Adolescent Psychiatric Clinic
Sophia Kinderziekenhuis
Gordelweg 160
3038 GE Rotterdam,
The Netherlands.

J.D. van der Ploeg. Professor at the Department of Education, Leiden University.

Centre for Special Education and Child Care
P.O. Box 9555
2300 RB Leiden,
The Netherlands.

M. Smit. Lecturer at the Department of Education, Leiden University.

Centre for Special Education and Child Care
P.O. Box 9555
2300 RB Leiden,
The Netherlands.

M. *van der Vall.* Professor of Social Research, Erasmus University at Rotterdam; Professor of Sociology, State University of New York at Buffalo.

Erasmus University
Department of Sociology
P.O. Box 1738
3000 DR Rotterdam,
The Netherlands.

H. Verzaal. Director and family therapist at 'Op Dreef', a residential treatment centre for adolescent girls in Amsterdam.

Op Dreef
Van Breestraat 162
1071 ZX Amsterdam,
The Netherlands.

A. Ward. Lecturer in Social Work, University of Reading

University of Reading
Faculty of Education and
Community Studies
Bulmershe Court
Reading RG6 1HY
United Kingdom.

F. Verhey. Child and adolescent psychiatrist at the child and adolescent psychiatric clinic, Sophia Children's Hospital, Erasmus University.

Child and Adolescent Psychiatric Clinic
Sophia Kinderziekenhuis
Gordelweg 160
3038 GE Rotterdam,
The Netherlands.

K. Visser. Lecturer and project manager at the Department of Social Work, Hogeschool van Amsterdam.

Hogeschool van Amsterdam
Department of Social Work
Singel 132-134
1015 AG Amsterdam,
The Netherlands.

T. Zandberg. Associate Professor at the Centre for the Education of Exceptional Children, University of Groningen.

Centre for the Education of Exceptional Children
Grote Rozenstraat 38
9712 TJ Groningen,
The Netherlands.